"From lives f̲   rity and relentless spirit   en have given us a most   ...g presentation in sharing the Gospel with Jews. The hallmark of "*Let's Witness to Jews--A Practical Guide for Sharing Your Faith*" is its simplicity and clarity.

George has personally brought many Jewish people to Christ, a number of which are now leaders in various Jewish ministries. They are the living proofs that his methods work and it is this that deserves a hearing when it comes to effectively witnessing to Jews. It is also the distinguishing feature that makes such a book 'different from all other books' in the field of Jewish evangelism."

Rev. Herbert Links
Drexel Hill, PA

"George Gruen is an anointed servant of the Lord. Over the past 33 years, since I first met him, I have seen him faithfully, steadfastly and single-mindedly witness to Jews and teach others to do the same. The resulting abundant fruit has been to the glory of God. In "*Let's Witness to Jews*," George and his wife, Jean, offer a very readable and practical guide for those who would like to learn to effectively present the Gospel to the Jew first and also to the Gentile. I recommend it highly."

Irving S. Wiesner, M.D.
Swathmore, PA

"This insightful book offers a wealth of Biblical guidance and practical advice for sharing your faith with sensitivity and understanding.

A must read for anyone seeking to be an effective witness to their Jewish and Gentile friends and contacts."

Dianna Shatley, Director of Missions Ministries, Brandywine Valley Baptist Church, Wilmington, DE

LET'S
WITNESS
to JEWS

An Individual or Small Group Study

LET'S
WITNESS
to JEWS

A Practical
Guide
for Sharing
Your Faith

GEORGE & JEAN GRUEN

TATE PUBLISHING & *Enterprises*

Published by Tate Publishing & Enterprises, LLC
127 E. Trade Center Terrace | Mustang, Oklahoma 73064 USA
1.888.361.9473 | www.tatepublishing.com

Tate Publishing is committed to excellence in the publishing industry. The company reflects the philosophy established by the founders, based on Psalm 68:11,
"The Lord gave the word and great was the company of those who published it."

Book design copyright © 2009 by Tate Publishing, LLC. All rights reserved.
Cover design by Kandi Evans
Interior design by Stephanie Woloszyn

Published in the United States of America

ISBN: 978-1-60799-260-8
1. Religion / Christian Ministry / General
2. Religion / Judaism / General
09.06.18

Authors' Notes

Unless otherwise noted, all Scripture quotations are from the King James Version of the Bible.

When quoting from the King James Version of the Bible, [ ] denotes explanation of scripture by authors. Occasionally ending punctuation and capitalization have also been changed to make it more readable.

In this study we will refer to the different branches of Judaism. A brief explanation of these divisions within Jewish worship will help your understanding of Jewish people and will assist you in learning how to share your faith.

Jews who worship as *Orthodox or Hasidic* will endeavor to keep the Law of Moses. They are very devout and will have faith in the God of Israel and usually will accept the Old Testament as their Bible. No unsaved Jews will accept what you quote or read from your New Testament. When you have shown Old Testament prophecy, then you can read the New Testament fulfillments in Jesus. As with Christians, they will believe in heaven. They do not believe in Hell. They admit that they sin but their sins can be forgiven by good deeds and asking God to forgive them. Their belief in Messiah is that he will come someday as a deliverer like Moses to free Israel from oppression. They do not believe Messiah is a member of the Godhead or Trinity. You will learn in our studies together how to show that Jesus is a member of the Godhead and that he has provided the blood of atonement for our sins to be forgiven. Jews have varying degrees of knowledge of the Old Testament but do not know the prophecies about Jesus. They will be surprised at your knowledge of their Bible and the prophecies you will share from the Old Testament.

Adherents to *Conservative Judaism* might not be as devout as the *Orthodox.* Their worship and faith is between the *Orthodox and Reform* groups. As you speak with Jews in this branch of Judaism, you will learn what each individual believes about spiritual matters. They might believe in heaven but not in Hell. Most will probably accept parts of the Old Testament as God's Word, but they will not know prophecy about Messiah. With the *Orthodox* and all branches of Judaism, *Conservatives* will know very little, if anything, of what true Christians believe. They are taught that Jesus is for the Gentiles and not for Jews. Most Jews believe that all Christians hate them. Your love in Christ Jesus will change this as you witness.

The Jewish people who are a part of the *Reform* group in Judaism might have little faith in God or the Bible. They will observe some Jewish holidays. They believe in living a "good life" with good deeds that will please people and God, if they believe there is a true God in heaven. Years ago there was a group of Jews in a *Reform* temple in a Midwest City. Their rabbi announced that he no longer believed in God and was going to resign as their rabbi. The congregation voted to keep him as their rabbi. This is just one case, but it reveals the spiritual need of these children of Abraham. Our studies will help you to show Jews who are atheists that the Bible is true.

The fourth group in Judaism is *Reconstructionism.* It began in Philadelphia, Pennsylvania in the 1900s as a movement in Judaism to adjust beliefs to modern times and society. They reinterpreted Jewish practices and observances. They do not believe in God but in being godly. They do not accept the authority of the Holy Scriptures.

There are Jewish people who are not active members of any congregation, but they still consider themselves to be Jewish. Judaism has not met their spiritual need, and they have discontinued attendance at regular services, except they might attend once or twice a year for the special holidays. Many Jews have inter-married with Gentiles of various branches of Christianity. These Jewish people might give opportunities for true Christians to share who Messiah Jesus is and how they can find forgiveness of sins through Jesus.

Most Jewish people, from my fifty-nine years of experience in Jewish evangelism, do not know true Bible believing Christians. They have never heard the Gospel in terminology that they can accept and still be Jewish. Their understanding of Christians comes from anti-Semitism, the Crusades, the Spanish Inquisition, pogroms (an organized persecution and massacre of a minority group, especially Jews), the Holocaust and constant derogatory remarks. My two sons, when they were boys, were called "dirty Jews" by a "so-called Christian" neighbor who attended a "Christian church." Jews need to meet true,

Bible-believing Christians who will show them love and share with them the Good News of salvation. This book will prepare you to be God's loving servant to reach needy Jewish hearts in your community. You will learn that you can do it, joyfully!

Dedication

To the Christians who love the Lord and desire to share their faith in Jesus with Jewish people and Gentiles; and to Jean, my dear wife, whose love and countless hours of work have made this book possible, I humbly dedicate it.

Table of Contents

Foreword

There are over fifteen million Jewish people in the world today. The Apostle Paul wrote "For I am not ashamed of the Gospel of Messiah, for it is the power of God to salvation to all who believe; to the Jew first, and also to the Gentile" Romans 1:16.

Jesus said "The fields are white unto harvest but the laborers are few. Pray therefore that the Lord of the harvest will send forth workers into his harvest field" Matthew 9:35–38. Jesus was speaking of the Jewish harvest field.

Few have answered this call over the centuries. Among those few is George Gruen. For almost sixty years, he has faithfully, sensitively, persistently, lovingly, and with great insight brought the truth that Jesus is the promised Jewish Messiah to his Jewish people.

It is one thing to proclaim the truth of the Gospel, but it is another thing to share it with Jewish people in a way that they can hear, understand and receive it. George Gruen has done just that.

I first met George when I was a teenager in the city of Philadelphia. He had a sports program of baseball and basketball. In order to play on the team, you had to attend a Bible study after the game. About fifteen of us Jewish boys were involved in his group. I was highly resistant to what was being taught and especially to the idea of Jesus being my Jewish Messiah. However, when I finally began to listen, I was amazed at what I was hearing as

George presented the Messianic prophecies from the Old Testament. He clearly, sensitively, patiently and persistently showed us that Jesus is the Jewish Messiah and Savior. George answered our questions and objections both scripturally and logically. Finally, I saw that Jesus was the One that our prophets foretold who would come to redeem all who would put their trust in Him.

It was through George Gruen's God-given expertise and the enlightenment of the Holy Spirit of God that I was born again and received Jesus as my Messiah and Savior. It was also through George's encouragement and life of a committed follower of Messiah Jesus that I was led to devote my life to bring this message of salvation to my Jewish people.

George Gruen with his wife Jean have now written a book that embodies the Biblical principles that he taught for so many years. God has used his ministry to literally bring hundreds of Jewish people to faith in Jesus as Messiah and Savior.

You too can be God's messenger to reach your Jewish friends by using the Scriptures, principles and techniques that are laid out for you in *Let's Witness to Jews.*

I recommend this book to you and pray that God will bless you as He promised to bless those that bless the Jewish people.

Rev. Abraham Sandler, Director
Awake O Israel Jewish Ministries
Philadelphia, PA

Introduction

Your new journey for the Lord begins today! When Christ Jesus saved us from our sins, he set us on a course for life that is to be exciting, joyful, and fulfilling as children of Almighty God. Have you discovered just what this walk through life should be for a Bible-believer? We have, and it is a joy to our hearts to share it with you.

Our association with many Christians who attended our seminars revealed a great need among God's people. We were challenged by the fact that many Bible-believers seldom, if ever, share their faith in Jesus with lost souls. The burden is there, but how to do it is not! Christians shy away from witnessing. They do not want to make a mistake and be a poor testimony for Jesus. Our new book, *Let's Witness to Jews,* is the answer to reaching out for Christ. The Lord will take your fears away and give you a blessed new life as you apply what you learn in this study. The Spirit of God will teach you and use you as you launch out for Jesus.

You will learn how to share your faith effectively with Jews and Gentiles. This is a very practical study that everyone can understand and put to use. As you go through the chapters, you will appreciate how the Bible verses can be applied in your sharing the gospel.

The Lord led us to write this book for a small group or individual study to assure you that you can witness. Our fifty-nine years of experience in witnessing is now yours! The methods we used in leading Jews and Gentiles to faith in Jesus are easily understood in the pages of *Let's Witness to Jews.* Yes they are! At your fingertips is the instruction you need. Everything is proven from the Bible. Your witness has a solid foundation! In the days ahead you will learn how to share the Trinity, why we know the Bible is true, how to use prophecy to prove Jesus is our Messiah and Savior, learn vital Bible verses about heaven and hell, how our sins are forgiven and the reality of true peace today and for eternity. It is thrilling to have such knowledge! It is wonderful to share it! Be ready for blessings from the Lord when you pray and witness.

If you have wondered why the Lord saved you, it will be made clear. If life is not very meaningful for you, that will change. When you complete and apply this study, your life will not be the same. Life will be worth living as a child of God in the will of God. Nothing can be better than this! We know, for it is our experience, and we pray it will be yours. God bless you.

—George and Jean Gruen

God's Gift—Our Responsibility

When a person accepts Jesus Christ as Savior, the joys of salvation become a part of his or her daily living. Nothing in this world can be compared to the peace that God gives to the believing heart. For the Bible-believer, death is not the end of life, but it is the doorway to heaven with eternal peace and joy in the presence of God. Along with all of the promises that the Lord has given to us that take us through the difficulties, hardships, and trials that we face, we are also given challenges and obligations.

Yes, Christians do have obligations to God. Salvation is free. Jesus Christ paid for our redemption. The Lord loves us and has provided everything for us. Even so, the Bible also tells believers that we, as children of God through Christ, have certain responsibilities. These instructions, obligations, and responsibilities apply to all of us because we are in the family of God. Let us consider some of these and how they should affect our lives.

In Genesis 12:1–3 we read,

Now the LORD had said unto Abram [later called Abraham], Get thee out of thy country, and from thy kindred, and from thy father's house, unto a land that I will show thee: And I will make of thee a great nation, and I will bless thee, and make thy name great; and thou shalt be a blessing: And I will bless them that bless thee,

and curse him that curseth thee: and in thee shall
all families of the earth be blessed.

Almighty God said that he would bless all families of
the earth through Abraham. How? As we study God's
Word, we see clearly that God would bless the people of
the earth through the descendants of Abraham who are
Hebrews or Jews. We learn from Old Testament prophecy
that, through the Jewish people, God would send to earth
the Messiah who would provide the way of forgiveness of
sin for all people.

Messiah took on human flesh. In Jesus' death on the
cross and in his resurrection, Jesus made possible for all
people the blood of atonement that God demanded for
sinners to be forgiven of their sins. In Leviticus 17:11 we
read, "For the life of the flesh is in the blood: and I have
given it to you upon the altar to make an atonement for
your souls: for it is the blood that maketh an atonement for
the soul." God's detailed instructions to Israel regarding the
Day of Atonement are given in Leviticus 16. This cleansing
of sin was effective in the lives of those who believed and
obeyed God's Word. We read in Leviticus 5:10, " … and the
priest shall make atonement for him for his sin which he
hath sinned, and it shall be forgiven him."

> Let the redeemed of the Lor d say so …
>
> Psalm 107:2

Today, we are not under the Old Testament law to obtain
the atonement. Christ Jesus fulfilled the law for us. John

1:29 clearly states this truth, "The next day John seeth Jesus coming unto him, and saith, Behold the Lamb of God, which taketh away the sin of the world." Forgiveness of our sins comes through faith in Jesus alone. We read in John 3:16, "For God so loved the world, that he gave his only begotten Son, that whosoever believeth in him should not perish, but have everlasting life."

In the New Testament, we read in John 4:21–22, "Jesus saith … salvation is of the Jews." This is a clear statement of Jesus that gives to us the fulfillment of the promise that God made to Abraham in Genesis 12:1–3. Jesus, on his human side, was of the lineage of Abraham. The blessings that God promised through Abraham are now effective in your life and mine through Christ Jesus! God's forgiveness of our sins is a reality in the Messiah. The peace and joy that we possess through faith in Jesus in this life and for eternity are wonderful!

> My mouth shall show forth thy righteousness and thy salvation all the day; for I know not the numbers thereof.
>
> Psalm 71:15

However, according to God's Word, all that he has given to us as his children places upon us responsibilities. What are we to do for the Lord from grateful hearts and our love for him? Is there a way in which we all can serve the Lord and share the burden for lost souls?

The children of Abraham, the Jews, for the most part

have strayed from the path that God laid out for them. As a nation, they did not accept Jesus as their Messiah and Redeemer; however, many individual Jews have put their trust in Jesus. How did they learn the truth that Jesus is their Messiah? A true Christian, or Bible-believer, shared the gospel with them in a way that they could understand and believe.

In Romans 10:1–4 and 10:12–14, we find God's desire for us today concerning the children of Israel.

> Brethren, my heart's desire and prayer to God for Israel is, that they might be saved. For I bear them record that they have a zeal of God, but not according to knowledge. For they being ignorant of God's righteousness, and going about to establish their own righteousness, have not submitted themselves unto the righteousness of God. For Christ is the end of the law for righteousness to every one that believeth … For there is no difference between the Jew and the Greek [Gentile]: for the same LORD over all is rich unto all that call upon him. For whosoever shall call upon the name of the Lord shall be saved. How then shall they call on him in whom they have not believed? And how shall they believe in him of whom they have not heard?

This is a heart-searching question for every Christian. How shall Jews and Gentiles believe when they have not really heard the way of salvation in Christ or Messiah Jesus? We all pray and that is essential to bringing lost souls to salvation. There is more to these verses than intercession. Someone shared the gospel with you and me. We believe and rejoice in our salvation.

The Lord now commands us to share his way of forgiveness of sin with others. Because God brought redemption to us through the descendants of Abraham in Jesus, the Lord expects us to give the gospel to the Jews as well as to the Gentiles. It is one of the imperatives in God's Word to us today. Christians are to witness to Jewish people!

Perhaps you feel that you do not know how to witness to Jews. The thought of audibly sharing your faith with a Jewish friend or contact brings apprehension or even fear. God will deliver you from all anxiety and give you confidence to witness. You will learn how to talk with Jews as we study together over the next twelve weeks. It is possible for you to effectively share God's Word. You can do it! Since 1950, we have been sharing the gospel with our Jewish people. Because of our experience, we can provide you with the information and preparation you need. Much joy awaits you as you use this material and share your faith with your Jewish contacts!

> Restore unto me the joy of thy salvation; and uphold me with thy free spirit. Then will I teach transgressors thy ways; and sinners shall be converted unto thee.
>
> Psalm 51:12–13

Another portion of Scripture is in Romans 11:30–31, which commands us to share our faith in Jesus with Jewish people. We read, "For as ye in times past have not believed God, yet have now obtained mercy through their unbelief: Even so have these also now not believed, that through your mercy they also may obtain mercy." After the gospel was given to the Jewish people, it then went to the Gentiles. Now, the Gentiles who believe the gospel and have obtained mercy and salvation from the Lord are to give the gospel to Jewish people so they also might trust in Jesus.

In Romans 1:16 we read, "For I am not ashamed of the gospel of Christ: for it is the power of God unto salvation to every one that believeth; to the Jew first, and also to the Greek [Gentiles]." In the book of Acts, we have the journeys of the Apostle Paul. When he went to a new community, he first spoke in the synagogue to give the gospel to his Jewish people. When the message was refused, he then turned to the Gentiles. In the next city that Paul visited, he again gave the Word of God to the Jews first and then to the Gentiles. The Lord, through the Apostle Paul, gave his message of salvation to the Hebrew people, and then the gospel was shared with Gentiles. Are Christians today to give the way of salvation to Gentile lost souls and neglect the Jewish people? No! God yearns for the descendants of Abraham to know his plan of redemption in Messiah Jesus. We must give them the opportunity to know Christ. You can effectively share the gospel with the Jews! The Lord will bless you as you witness to the children of Israel.

As you are burdened to share your faith with Jewish and Gentile friends and contacts, the Lord will give you the words to speak. God will always, by his Spirit, encourage us through his Word. When God gives us a task to do, he will also give us the ability to do it! Another promise to help us share our faith is in 2 Timothy 1:7–8,

> For God hath not given us the spirit of fear; but of power, and of love, and of a sound mind. Be not thou therefore ashamed of the testimony of our Lord … but be thou partaker of the afflictions of the gospel according to the power of God; Who hath saved us, and called us with an holy calling, not according to our works, but according to his own purpose and grace, which was given us in Christ Jesus before the world began.

Can there be greater promises than these? The Lord will take away our fears! God will give us power, which is the physical strength we need. He will give us love to overcome difficulties. The Lord will give us a sound mind, or the knowledge we need, to witness and answer questions. This sustaining work of the Lord in our lives will rid us of all of our nervousness and anxiety. In place of these hindering thoughts, we will have confidence because Almighty God will work through us! There is great joy in the hearts of all God's children after they have had the opportunity to make known the gospel to lost souls. As we go through these studies, you will be prepared to share your faith with Jewish people as well as with Gentiles. There are different words to use when witnessing to Jewish people. Jews have obstacles to placing their faith in Jesus because of the persecution they have endured. Our studies will teach you what to say and what not to say when sharing with Jews. The principles you will learn will enable you to touch all lost souls.

God also says that we should not be ashamed to speak for him. There might be opposition when we witness, but that is part of serving the Lord Jesus. Jesus went to the cross to save us from our sins. Almighty God raised Jesus from the dead by his power. Now God will help us to be his ambassadors by his mighty power. The Lord will enable us to be what he wants us to be to reach lost souls with his plan of salvation.

> O Lor d, open thou my lips; and my mouth shall show forth thy praise.
>
> Psalm 51:15

Yes, you might have anxiety or fear when you first begin to share, but Jesus knows this and he will give you the words to speak. We know this is true. In all our years of witnessing, the Lord has given us the words to give the way of salvation to needy hearts. You might say, "But I am very shy, and it is hard for me to speak." Yes, we know the feeling! As new believers, we were very shy and felt that we could never talk to anyone about the gospel. This all changed when we let God work in our hearts and then he worked through us.

George accepted Jesus as his Savior when he was a

boy. He attended Sunday school, church, prayer meeting and was active in the youth group. He followed the Lord in baptism. When he was eighteen years of age, a new experience changed his life forever. The Christian and Missionary Alliance held a youth conference at their campus at Nyack, New York, which George attended. The evangelist challenged the young people from Romans 12:1–2,

> I beseech you therefore, brethren, by the mercies of God, that ye present your bodies a living sacrifice, holy, acceptable unto God, which is your reasonable service. And be not conformed to this world: but be ye transformed by the renewing of your mind, that ye may prove what is that good, and acceptable, and perfect, will of God.

God spoke to George's heart, and he felt the call of the Lord to dedicate his life and future to the will of his Savior. He argued with the Lord and said, "I am a shy and quiet teenager, you cannot use me. I am too bashful and cannot speak to lost souls." At the conclusion of the service an altar call was given with the challenge for teenagers to give their lives completely to God for His will. With many other young people, he went forward and stood before the Lord at the front of that meeting place. He spoke to his Savior from his heart: "Lord, I'm shy, bashful and don't know if you can use me. I do not know if I can talk to people, but here I am. If you can use me, I am willing, Lord. Take my life and direct me for your glory." George meant this commitment to the Lord with all his heart.

From that day, August 8, 1946, at about 9:00 p.m., George has seen the Lord work in his life until this present hour. The Lord led him to Bible school where he prepared for full-time Christian ministry. At school, he answered the call for students to work among Jewish people in the Bronx, New York. After graduation in 1950, God called him to full-time Jewish evangelism at the Bronx Messianic Center of The Christian and Missionary Alliance in New York. Doris joined him as his wife in September 1950 and they served at the Center until October, 1953. In a miraculous way, God moved the Gruens to Philadelphia, Pennsylvania to open a witness to Jewish young people. The Lord blessed this ministry and Jewish teen-agers, young adults and older people put their faith in Christ Jesus for salvation. Two of the Jewish young men went on to Bible college and worked in ministries among their Jewish people.

In September, 1954, George was ordained to the ministry with The Christian and Missionary Alliance. Rev. George Gruen served with The C & M A for 28 years in Jewish work. Then God led him to go full-time with the radio outreach, Truth for Israel, Inc., that he began in 1962. The past 47 years have seen a world-wide ministry that is reaching Jewish people in over 80 countries and throughout the United States by the Internet, radio broadcasts, literature, CDs and conducting seminars on how Christians can effectively witness to the children of Israel.

There have been trials, illness, opposition, and anxious

moments; however, they were followed by answers to prayer and a glorious victory in Christ! What joy there is in giving the gospel to lost souls. How thrilling it is to see the peace of salvation on the face of a new believer who heard the gospel through our witness! What an awesome privilege it is to serve Almighty God and see him work through us to bring souls to salvation in Christ Jesus.

Our commitment to the Lord's plan for our lives is what he expects of each of us. Oh yes, dear one in Christ, it is worth it to say "yes" to God's call upon your life and to experience his leading and direction day by day! Every Christian should have this experience of commitment to serve the Lord and give his plan of salvation to lost souls. You can make this decision to have the Lord take over, guide, and direct in your life as a homemaker, a worker in any type of job, a business person, a professional man or woman, a retiree, an elderly person, or a teenager. Age is not the deciding factor. Your will is!

The Spirit of God on the day of Pentecost gave the early believers power to share the gospel. The Lord, by his Holy Spirit, will use your voice too. You can know the joy of commitment to God, as well as the peace and happiness that comes when we share his Word as God opens the way. You can know and experience the wonder of seeing God's Spirit work in Jewish and Gentile hearts to bring them to salvation in Jesus.

Let us say with Isaiah in Isaiah 6:8–9, "Also I heard the voice of the Lord, saying, Whom shall I send, and who will go for us? Then said I, Here am I; send me. And he [God] said, Go, and tell this people ... "

Making It Personal

1. Is prayer and living the Christian life sufficient for a believer to see a lost soul come to faith in Jesus for salvation? Explain your answer.

2. Does God expect every Christian to audibly share their faith in Jesus? Why?

3. How can a Christian learn to witness to Jews?

4. Does a believer witness to Jews the same way and with the same methods and terminology as they do to Gentiles? Why?

5. Do you feel confident to share your faith with your Jewish friends? Practice sharing your faith now with someone in your group or have a friend listen to you.

6. Are only missionaries, pastors, and full-time Christian workers supposed to witness to Jewish and Gentile people? Is this found in the Holy Scriptures? Where?

7. If no one shared the gospel with you, would you have salvation and the assurance that you are going to heaven when you die?

Additional Bible Verses for Study

- Philippians 4:13
- Isaiah 40:25–31

- Acts 4:18–20, 4:31
- Romans 10
- Romans 11:1–5, 11:11–14
- 2 Corinthians 5:8–10, 5:14–20

Terminology when Witnessing

The gospel must be shared with Jewish people in a way that they can understand. Jews have suffered greatly throughout history. Their suffering and deaths have often come at the hands of so-called Christians. These unsaved people speak of God, Christ, and Jesus and then foster anti-Semitism. Millions of Jewish people have died at the hands of those who have called themselves Christians. The horrors of Hitler's Holocaust, when six million Jewish men, women, and children were murdered, put into focus the depth of the suffering of the children of Israel. George's uncle Herman was killed in the Holocaust at the Buchenwald Camp in World War II in Germany. As we keep in mind these atrocities, we will understand why it is necessary to be careful in the words we use to share the gospel with the children of Israel.

> But sanctify the Lord God in your hearts: and be ready always to give an answer to every man that asketh you a reason of the hope that is in you …
>
> 1 Peter 3:15

The walls of prejudice that have been built over the years must be broken down so that we might have open lines of communication with our Jewish contacts. It is also vital that we understand some of the problems that Jewish people face when they consider the gospel. We will share with you words to use and words not to use when giving God's plan of redemption to Jews.

In Colossians 4:5–6 the Lord gives instruction to us as we share our faith in Jesus. God says, "Walk in wisdom toward them that are without, redeeming the time. Let your speech be always with grace, seasoned with salt, that ye may know how ye ought to answer every man." The Spirit of God will give us wisdom to answer the questions that are asked by seeking hearts. In sharing your faith, you will meet Jewish people who honestly desire to know God. Unlike you or me, they have never met a person who has a personal relationship with the God of Israel. You will also be confronted by Jews whose hearts are not open to God's truth. The Lord will give you wisdom and discernment.

In the more than fifty-nine years that we have spent in reaching the Jewish people with the gospel, we have found the following terminology to be helpful.

1. LORD JESUS CHRIST

It is difficult for Jewish people to hear the words "Lord Jesus Christ." We, of course, believe in the Lord Jesus Christ. He is a member of the Godhead and our Savior. However, when we say Lord Jesus to Jews, they believe we accept Christ Jesus as God. To the Jewish mind, we are idolaters for we worship more than one eternal God. Judaism teaches its people that there is only one

God, and he is the God of Abraham, Isaac, and Jacob or the God of Israel. They do not accept Messiah Jesus as God. We must explain to them what the Old Testament teaches about the Godhead and how the God of Israel has revealed himself to us as three eternal beings and yet one God. The study of the Godhead will be covered in the next chapter where we will see what the Bible teaches about the God of Israel. You will be surprised what the Bible reveals. You will learn how to explain to Jews and Gentiles that Messiah Jesus is in the Godhead and is God according to Hebrew Scripture.

> But ye shall receive power, after that the Holy Spirit is come upon you: and ye shall be witnesses unto me both in Jerusalem, and in all Judea, and in Samaria, and unto the uttermost part of the earth.
>
> Acts 1:8

Jews also have difficulty in talking about Christ. Perhaps it is because of Christ being a part of the word Christian. It is better to say Messiah rather than Christ when sharing with unsaved Jews. The words Christ and Messiah both mean Anointed One.

2. CHRISTIAN

Early in our ministry, we called ourselves Bible-believers rather than Christians. If you call yourself a Christian, you identify yourself with those so-called or false Christians who have persecuted and murdered Jews throughout history. Saying Christian will make an effective witness very difficult, even when you try to explain who is a true Christian. Without using the word Christian, stress your love for Jewish people because of what Jews have done for you in giving you God's Word in the Bible. In the Bible, we learn of God's way for us to be forgiven of our sins through the atonement provided by Messiah. It would be better as you begin to share just to say Messiah, rather than Messiah Jesus, until you have had time to read Isaiah 53 and explain it. Our study of Isaiah 53 and prophecy will be in a future chapter.

> O God, thou hast taught me from my youth: and hitherto have I declared thy wondrous works. Now also when I am old … O God, forsake me not; until I have showed thy strength unto this generation, and thy power to every one that is to come.
>
> Psalm 71:17–18

Is it really necessary not to use the word Christian in witnessing? In 2005, a sixteen-year-old Jewish boy in Baltimore, Maryland, asked a sixteen-year-old true Bible-believing girl who was sharing God's Word with him, "Why do Christians hate me?" He must have had contact with people he thought were Christians who used derogatory remarks about him because he is a Jew.

After many months of this Christian girl's witness to him and showing him the love of God, he said that he had never seen such love for Jews come from a Gentile or Christian.

Some so-called Christians approve of the Holocaust saying that the six million Jewish men, women, and children deserved to be murdered and the Holocaust was a collective punishment for Jews. So-called Christians do not speak for true, Bible-believing people of God. Jews, however, do not know the difference until we, in love, share the Word of God with them and live Jesus before them.

3. CHURCH

Rather than speaking of your church, refer to it as the place where I study the Bible and learn about God. Just to mention church associates you with the murder of Jewish people. In the Spanish Inquisition in a d 1400s, Jews were given the choice of renouncing Judaism and joining the church or they would be put to death. Thousands died! Other Jews joined the church to save their lives. The pages of history are stained with the blood of Jews who suffered and were killed by those who professed to follow Christ Jesus and the church but were not true believers in him. You can readily understand why you should refrain from using the word "church." You might meet a Jewish person who has had much contact with true, loving Bible-believers and understands what a true church teaches. In such situations, you could tell them where you go to church. Until a Jewish person knows the difference and shares this with you, it would be good to say you go to a place where there are services to learn about God. The Lord will guide you.

4. CROSS

To the Jewish person, the cross is a symbol of anti-Semitism. When crusaders marched through Europe to Jerusalem in the eleventh to the end of the thirteen centuries, multitudes of Jews lost their lives and their villages were destroyed. This was done under the symbol of the cross which they had on their lances and clothing. Never wear a cross of any type when witnessing to Jewish people. To the Jews, the cross means persecution and death. Rather than saying the cross, just speak of Messiah Jesus dying to provide the blood of atonement that we might be forgiven of our sins. Jewish people have been blamed for the death of Jesus. As we know, we are all responsible for his sacrifice for us. It states in Isaiah 53:10, "Yet it pleased the LORD to bruise him…" We know God planned the death of Jesus for him to be the blood of atonement for the cleansing of our sins.

5. CONVERT

Jews resent people who want to convert them to faith in Christ, Christianity and the church. From our study, you can readily understand why this is true. It is not our purpose to change one's religion or to convert them from a synagogue or temple to a church. Our desire is for both Jews and Gentiles to have a right relationship with the Almighty God of Israel through faith in Messiah Jesus. In the Messiah, we find the way to be forgiven of our sins and have new life with true peace, joy, fulfillment, and a wonderful future before us according to God's promises in the Bible. After people put their faith in God's plan for their lives in Messiah Jesus, the Spirit of God will lead them to the right place to worship for spiritual life and growth.

> Finally, my brethren, be strong in the Lord, and in the power of his might ... And your feet shod with the preparation of the gospel of peace ... taking the shield of faith ... Praying always ... And for me, that utterance may be given unto me, that I may open my mouth boldly, to make known the mystery of the gospel ...
>
> Ephesians 6:10–19

If the word convert is mentioned in your conversations, use the illustration of King David of Israel. In Psalm 51:3 and 51:10–13, we find King David talking about converting. We read in Psalm 51:12–13, "Restore unto me the joy of thy salvation; and uphold me with thy free spirit. Then will I teach transgressors thy ways; and sinners shall be converted unto thee." What does God's Word through King David of Israel say to us? The salvation of God brings joy by his Spirit in us. Since King David knew this great joy, he would teach sinners the way to be forgiven of their sins, and then sinners would be converted from sin to righteousness and God's will for their lives. This was good enough for King David of Israel, and it is good enough for me! Judaism teaches that people should not share their faith and try to convert others; however, this is not what the Old Testament teaches. It is not to change people from one religion to another, but from living in sin to living for God and righteousness. In older Jewish versions of the Bible, the word "converted" was used in Psalm 51:13. In newer Jewish Bibles and some other versions, the word is translated "be brought back to." That would mean for people to be brought back from living in sin to living in God's will.

6. TRINITY

It is better to say Godhead rather than Trinity. Trinity is associated with Christianity and the church and might cause Jewish people to turn away from you and the ability for you to share God's Word.

7. MISSIONARY

To the Jewish people, a missionary is a Christian who wants to convert Jews from Judaism to Christianity to worship the Lord Jesus Christ in a church and possibly before a cross. Need I say more? When you desire to share any of our Bible materials with your Jewish friend, just say, "I know this Jewish man who has a relationship with the God of Israel that has given him great peace. He sent, or gave, me this leaflet that he wrote. I'll leave it with you and when I see you again let me know what you think about it." Place the leaflet or article on a table and leave. If you have to hand it to him or her, silently pray that it will be accepted. (Please see our contact information at the end of this book for information on ordering tracts and CDs for Jews.)

8. SAVED—REDEEMED

These are common words used in church and among true Christians. It is better not to use them with unsaved people but rather say, "God has forgiven my sins. I know I am going to heaven when I die and I want to share this plan of the God of Israel with you."

9. OLD TESTAMENT—NEW TESTAMENT

In conversations with Jewish people, we do not say Old Testament. If you do, it is possible that it will turn the person away. Usually the old is not as valuable as the new. People get rid of the old when they obtain the new. Rather than speaking of the Old Testament, say the Jewish Bible or the Jewish Holy Scriptures. Many people, when sharing with a Jewish person, will not say the New Testament but rather the New Covenant. You might say something like "The prophesy in the Jewish Bible that

God gave through the Jewish man, Isaiah, in chapter 53 is fulfilled in the record of the New Covenant." It also depends on how much knowledge the inquirer has and just how much he or she will accept. The Lord will guide you when to say New Testament.

> Fear thou not; for I am with thee: be not dismayed; for I am thy God: I will strengthen thee; yea, I will help thee; yea, I will uphold thee with the right hand of my righteousness. For I the Lor d thy God will hold thy right hand, saying unto thee, Fear not; I will help thee.
>
> Isaiah 41:10, 41:13

When sharing your faith with Jewish people, you will find that they have many different beliefs just as when you share your faith with a Gentile who attends a Lutheran, Methodist, etc. church. Those who call themselves an Orthodox or Conservative Jew will have the most faith in God and the Jewish Bible. However, many Jews are atheists or agnostics. Sharing with those who attend places of worship called Reform or Reconstructionist, or who do not attend any Jewish services, will be different from when you share with someone who calls himself an Orthodox or a Conservative Jew. These branches of Judiasm were explained in the beginning of this book under "Author's Notes." For further detail, see the chapter called Understanding the Faith of Jewish People. Become familiar with Jewish terminology so that you can be a more effective witness to Jewish people. The Spirit of God will guide you as you speak to touch hearts with God's Word. Unsaved souls need to know the way of salvation through Messiah Jesus and this will be accomplished as we faithfully present the gospel to Jews and Gentiles.

Making It Personal

1. Do the experiences that unsaved Jews have been through need to be considered as we share the gospel? How have these experiences effected Jews?

2. Do you witness to Jews the same as Gentiles? Share the differences or similarities.

3. Should we speak of the Lord Jesus Christ in our sharing with Jewish people? What problem might hinder your witness? When speaking of Christ Jesus, it would be better to use what words?

4. Should we use the term Christian with Jews? If not, why not, and what should we call ourselves?

5. How do Jews feel about the church? How do we explain the church to inquirers?

6. We rejoice in the cross on which Christ Jesus died for our sins to be forgiven. Do Jewish people have any problem with talking about the cross? Why? If so, what else can we say rather than the cross?

7. Why should you not use the word convert or converted when sharing God's plan for our lives?

What Scripture in the Old Testament explains converting?

8. What words can best describe the Old Testament when talking with Jews? Should you say New Testament?

9. What experience have you had in sharing your faith with Jewish people?

Additional Bible Verses for Study

- Matthew 28:18–20

- Luke 24:46–48

- Romans 1:8

- Revelation 3:20–22

Understanding the Godhead

Christians can effectively share the gospel with the Jewish people in their communities, at businesses, or with those who have married into their family. After one of our seminars on how to share the Word of God with the children of Israel, two grandmothers told us that their grandchildren had married Jewish unbelievers. They said that the information they learned at the seminars helped them to understand how Jewish people feel about spiritual things and would assist them in sharing God's Word with their Jewish relatives.

In this chapter, we will answer questions that are often asked by Jews regarding the Godhead. Regardless of whether the Jewish person is Orthodox, Conservative, Reform, or in some other group, they believe they cannot accept Jesus, for in so doing they would be idolaters. They recognize that Jesus is in the Trinity as far as the Christian faith is concerned, but they cannot place their trust in this teaching. They believe only in one God. Jews are taught that if they trust in Jesus, they will worship two Gods and be involved in idolatry. The answer to this objection to Jesus' deity is found in the Old Testament. The Jewish Holy Scriptures clearly teach that God has manifested himself to us as three eternal beings.

> And unto the Jews I became as a Jew, that I might gain the Jews … that I might by all means save some.
>
> 1 Corinthians 9:20, 9:22

If Jews believe in God, and many do, they do not know what their Bible teaches about who God is and how he has revealed himself to us. The Godhead—Father, Messiah/Son, and Holy Spirit—has never been explained to them. We must clearly present this vital foundation for faith so they can understand the full plan of God for their lives for today and eternity.

As you share the following verses of Scripture, do so slowly. Do not rush, but give time for each truth to be understood and accepted. Romans 10:17 states, "So then faith cometh by hearing, and hearing by the Word of God." It is the Word of God that will bring conviction as the Spirit of God moves upon hearts.

Our study begins with the very first verse in the Bible, Genesis 1:1, "In the beginning God created the heaven and the earth."

This verse is very familiar to most people. God created everything. This is a simple statement of truth, but there is more in this verse for us concerning Almighty God. The Godhead is here in this verse when we understand the Hebrew word for God and how it is translated in the Bible. The Hebrew word for God in the singular is *El* (used about 220 times as in Genesis 14:18) or *Elah* (about ninety times as in Daniel 2:28) in the

Old Testament. Neither of these Hebrew words, *El* or *Elah,* is in Genesis 1:1. The Hebrew for God in this verse is *Elohim* (pronounced L—O—Heem with a long e). When "im" is added to a Hebrew word, it makes it plural. The literal translation of Genesis 1:1 from the Hebrew is, "In the beginning Gods created the heaven and the earth." *Yes, Gods!* This Hebrew word, *Elohim,* is found over 2,500 times in the Old Testament! It is Gods and yet one God—a unity or the Godhead. *Elohim* is also used when referring to heathen gods.

Can we be certain that Gods is what the Almighty God of Israel is saying to us in Genesis 1:1? In 2 Kings 17:29 we read, "Howbeit every nation made gods of their own..." Many nations, plural, made gods or idols, plural—more than one single god. In the context, this is the correct translation. What is the Hebrew word in 2 Kings 17:29 from which gods is translated? It is *Elohim*— the same Hebrew word used for God in Genesis 1:1.

> Holding forth the word of life; that I may rejoice in the day of Christ, that I have not run in vain, neither laboured in vain.
>
> Philippians 2:16

In Exodus 20, we have the Ten Commandments. In verse one and two, we have God speaking. This is the God of Israel as the text clearly reveals, for he brought Israel out of bondage. The Hebrew word from which God is translated is *Elohim.* In the context, this is correct.

Almighty God is then speaking again to us in verse three where we read, "Thou shalt have no other gods before me." The Hebrew word from which gods is translated in verse three is *Elohim*. Since this refers to many people worshipping false idols, it is correctly translated gods.

The context determines whether *Elohim* should be translated God or gods. Our Almighty God is revealed to us in more than one single deity in the Bible. The God of the Holy Scriptures speaks to us as our heavenly Father, as the Messiah, and thirdly as the Holy Spirit. The following verses in the Old Testament will enumerate this great truth.

All three members of the Godhead are given in one verse. Say to your Jewish friend, "I am going to read a verse from your Bible. Let me know what this says to you. It is in the God-inspired writings of the Jewish man of God, Isaiah." Then read Isaiah 48:16, "Come ye near unto me, hear ye this; I have not spoken in secret from the beginning; from the time that it was, there am I …" Then ask, "Who is speaking in this verse?" Of course, God is, for no human person has been from the beginning. When you have established that God is speaking, then continue reading the verse. It says, "And now the LORD God, and his Spirit, hath sent me." The speaker, who is an eternal one or God, then speaks of the LORD God, a second deity, and then his Spirit, a third deity.

We now have the LORD God and his Spirit (the Spirit of God is certainly of the Godhead) sending the speaker who is God! There are three members of the Godhead mentioned in this verse of the Bible. You can then read the next verse in this chapter to prove that God is speaking in verse 16. Isaiah 48:17 reads, "Thus saith the LORD, thy Redeemer, the Holy One of Israel; I am the LORD thy God [a form of *Elohim*] which teacheth thee to profit, which leadeth thee by the way that thou shouldest go."

Another prophecy in the Jewish Holy Scriptures concerning the coming of the Messiah also reveals to us that the Messiah is God. In Jeremiah 23:5–6 we read,

> Behold, the days come, saith the LORD, that I will raise unto David a righteous Branch, and a King shall reign and prosper, and shall execute judgment and justice in the earth. In his days Judah shall be saved, and Israel shall dwell safely: and this is the name whereby he shall be called, THE LORD OUR RIGHTEOUSNESS.

Orthodox Jews wait for the coming of the Messiah who would be a descendant of King David. Their Messiah will bring peace to Israel and the Jewish people. Rabbis give the name of branch, root, sprout, or shoot in Jewish versions of the Scriptures to the one sent from God in these verses who is the Messiah. In Jewish teaching, the Messiah will not be God but will be a great deliverer and ruler such as Moses.

When you read LORD (all capitals) in your Bible, it is a translation of four Hebrew consonants, YHVH, that give us the name of God that he is the self-existent one—the eternal I AM who reveals himself. Jewish people do not pronounce this holy name of deity, nor do they write it. Bible translators will use LORD for YHVH. Initially when vowels were put to these consonants for pronunciation, this name of deity is JEHOVAH. It is the name of God used for his redemptive acts and covenants. In Jewish translations of the Holy Scriptures, they will not use LORD but Lord when they have YHVH in the Hebrew.

> For it is God which worketh in you both to will and to do of his good pleasure...ye shine as lights in the world.
>
> Philippians 2:13, 2:15

What does Jeremiah 23:5–6 tell us about Almighty God and the Messiah? The LORD, Jehovah, is speaking. He foretells that he will send one to reign on earth who, on his human side, will be a descendant of King David of Israel. This one's reign will be with judgment, justice, and prosperity in the earth. When he, who is the Messiah, reigns, Judah and Israel (this would be the Jewish people) will live in peace and safety. Then the LORD tells us the name that this one will be called! His name is "THE LORD OUR RIGHTEOUSNESS" or "JEHOVAH OUR RIGHTEOUSNESS." God in heaven sends to earth a member of the Godhead to defeat the enemies of Israel and bring peace to the world. Jews and Gentiles will know that this one is God on earth because of his power and reign! God the Father is in heaven and the one sent is the Messiah as these verses and others in the

Bible clearly foretell. This coming of the Messiah to rule the world in peace is yet future as I write this book. In another chapter in this book, I will give the details of this coming of the Messiah. Orthodox Jews look forward to this great event. It will happen in God's time as the Jewish Holy Scriptures promise.

The key verse in Judaism is Deuteronomy 6:4, "Hear, O Israel: The LORD our God is one LORD." This is the statement of Jewish people that they believe in one God and not in many Gods as they say Christians believe. What does Deuteronomy 6:4 say? The Hebrew word for "our God" in this verse is a form of *Elohim*—the plural for God.

The word for "one" in this verse in Hebrew is *echad*. The word *echad* can mean a unity of more than one. If God wanted to say a definite single person, the word for a single one in Hebrew is *yachid*. We have already seen in Jewish Scriptures that the Messiah is one in the Godhead as is the Spirit of God. *Echad* in Hebrew is three letters. These same three letters are used in other places in the Old Testament to mean unity, solidarity, unite, and combine. In Deuteronomy 6:4, *echad* teaches us that there is more than a single one in the Godhead.

To illustrate the use of *echad* in the Scriptures, we read in Genesis 2:24, "Therefore shall a man leave his father and his mother, and shall cleave unto his wife: and they shall be one flesh." This very familiar Scripture shows us what *echad* can mean. The word for one in this verse is the Hebrew *echad*. We have two people, a man and a woman, who are united in marriage. In the marriage act,

Let's Witness to Jews

they become one flesh. Are they still two people? Yes, and yet they are one or a unity. This is a human illustration, but it shows how in *echad* there is more than one person. In the Godhead, we have *echad*—one—and yet there are three divine ones: God the Father, God the Messiah, and God the Holy Spirit as the Bible reveals to us.

Jewish people have a prayer book known as the *Siddur*. It is used for the Jewish holidays and for services. One of the principles talks about the Creator being a Unity. This is an amazing statement in the Jewish prayer book! It says that God is a Unity spelled with a capital *U*. No explanation is given for this, but we know the statement is true as we have seen in our study of the Godhead. Unfortunately, in a newer version, it has been changed to read God is one, and not a Unity, so that it conforms to the present teaching in Judaism.

We read in Genesis 1:2, 1:26, 3:22,

> And the earth was without form, and void; and darkness was upon the face of the deep. And the spirit of God (*Elohim*) moved upon the face of the waters. And God (*Elohim*) said, Let us make man in our image, after our likeness … And the LORD God (Jehovah *Elohim*) said, Behold, the man is become as one of us, to know good and evil …

These verses in Genesis referring to God's creation of the world clearly reveal the Godhead. They show us the Spirit of God in creation in Genesis 1:2. When speaking of the creation of man, *Elohim* says "let us"—plural, more than one divine being created man in Genesis 1:26. Then in Genesis 3:22 the plurality of God is given when he refers to himself as us.

Newer versions of the Jewish Bible change Genesis 1:26 to read, "And God said, I will make man in my image" to say God is singular and not plural. A footnote is given to say that in some versions it does say, "Let us … our likeness."

As we have considered these various verses in our Old Testament, we know Almighty God has revealed himself to us as the Godhead, or the Trinity—God the Father, God the Messiah, and God the Holy Spirit. We will see in our studies how Almighty God provides the way for Jewish and Gentile men and women to be forgiven of their sins and know true peace in this life and for eternity.

Making It Personal

1. What does it mean when the New Testament says, "Unto the Jews I became as a Jew, that I might gain the Jews … that I might by all means save some"?

2. What do Jewish people believe about God?

3. Why is it important to know what the Hebrew word for God is and means in Genesis 1:1?

4. What does Genesis 1:1, 1:26 and 3:22 teach us about God?

Let's Witness to Jews

5. How would you explain what Isaiah 48:16–17 teaches about the Godhead?

6. What do we learn about the Messiah from Jeremiah 23:5–6?

7. What is the key verse in the Old Testament that Jews believe tells them that there is only one God? What does "echad" mean in this verse?

8. What is the Jewish prayer book?

Additional Bible Verses for Study

- Isaiah 9:6–7
- Zechariah 9:9, 12:8–10, 14:1–5

The Two Comings of Messiah

Orthodox Jews look for the coming of the Messiah. The Messiah for whom they pray is not the Messiah whom we know from Bible prophecy. Orthodox Jews seek a Messiah who will deliver them from the oppression of those people who seek the destruction of Israel, Judaism, and the Jewish people. They do not see Messiah as one of the Godhead, but as a great human deliverer such as Moses. Their hope is that this Messiah will defeat the enemies of Israel and bring lasting peace. Since Jesus did not bring political peace to the Jewish people, and they have suffered through the past 2,000 years, Jews say that Jesus cannot be the Messiah. This is the main Jewish argument against Jesus being their promised Messiah. When you explain from the Bible that the God of Israel sends the Messiah two times to earth for two different reasons, it will help Jewish people to see that Jesus is the Messiah of Israel and our Redeemer.

> We have also a more sure word of prophecy; whereunto ye do well that ye take heed, as unto a light that shineth in a dark place, unto the day dawn, and the day star arise in your hearts … For the prophecy came not in old time by the will of man: but holy men of God spake as they were moved by the Holy Spirit.
>
> 2 Peter 1:19, 1:21

You will meet many Jewish people who know nothing about the Messiah. They have no opinion about Messiah. If they are of the Reform Jewish faith, or attend other liberal places of worship, they might believe that conditions in the world will get better and better through human endeavor until humanity reaches a Messianic Era of world peace. Those who accept this teaching need to hear what the Bible says about the Jewish Messiah. When they know what the Holy Scriptures say, they will be in a position to make correct judgments concerning who the Messiah is and their need to know him as their Redeemer. If hearts are willing to accept the truth as given in the Bible, they will have the foundation they need to believe in the true Messiah of God. Someone must share the Word of God with them. The Lord has given to you and to us this great responsibility and privilege.

The average Jewish person has little or no knowledge about what the Bible teaches in prophecy regarding the coming of the Messiah. Since many Jewish men and women, as well as Gentiles, have no hope or faith in God and the Holy Scriptures, they live only for the material possessions of this world. They devote their time and energies in the pursuit of success and happiness for their lives and for their families. Because of the hypocrisy they have seen in religion including so-called Christianity, they have no basis for faith in God or the Bible. Anti-Semitism also contributes toward the lack of faith in the lives of so many Jewish hearts. Many Jews feel, "How can I believe in Jesus when his followers persecute me and my Jewish people?" The children of Israel have just cause for their lack of faith, but it can be overcome. They need to know the truth of God in the Bible from loving, Bible-believers. You can do it!

In reaching out to Jewish people, it is necessary to help them understand what the Old Testament says about the two comings of the Messiah to earth. The Bible is very clear in revealing to us that the Messiah will come from God to earth the first time to bring personal peace. This peace is available to all who will put their faith in God's plan for the forgiveness of their sins. After Messiah has accomplished the way of salvation for Jews and Gentiles, he returns to heaven and is seated at the right hand of God. Messiah is there until God's appointed time for him to come the second time to earth to bring peace to Israel and the world. This second coming will happen in the future.

THE FIRST COMING OF MESSIAH TO EARTH

1. *Messiah will come to earth and take on a human body to accomplish God's plan of salvation for Jews and Gentiles.*

How will Messiah come to earth? What do the Jewish prophets foretell in the Holy Scriptures? We will consider a number of these prophecies beginning with Isaiah 7:14, "Therefore the Lord himself shall give you a sign; Behold, a virgin shall conceive, and bear a son, and shall call his name Immanuel."

This is a well-known verse of Scripture to Bible-believers. However, Jewish people have never read it. They do not know what this wonderful Scripture says concerning the Messiah's first coming. We must share it with them. It was written by Isaiah who is one of the greatest Jewish men of God to record the Word of God in the Holy Scriptures. The God of Israel gave, through Isaiah, many of the prophecies about the coming of the Messiah. Isaiah 7:14 gives us many truths about his first coming.

> Who hath ascended up into heaven, or descended?
> who hath gathered the wind in his fists?
> who hath bound the waters in a garment?
> who hath established all the ends of the earth?
> what is his name, and what is his son's name, if thou canst tell?
>
> Proverbs 30:4

The Holy Spirit of Almighty God would, in a miraculous way, make this Jewish virgin conceive and give birth to a perfect, sinless baby. There would be no human father to pass on the sin that comes to all human beings from Adam. Jewish teachers say that the word virgin in Isaiah 7:14 is not correct. They say the translation should be young woman. The Hebrew word for young woman, that can also mean a virgin, is *bethulah.* The Hebrew word *bethulah* is not found in Isaiah 7:14. The Hebrew word used in this verse is *almah* and is correctly translated virgin. *Almah* occurs only seven times in the Old Testament and in the context, every verse definitely means virgin. The references are: Genesis 24:43, Exodus 2:8, Proverbs 30:19, Psalm 68:26, Song of Solomon 1:3, 6:8, and Isaiah 7:14.

Jewish or Hebrew translators of the Bible in the third century bc knew that *almah* meant virgin. Seventy Hebrew (Jewish) scholars translated the Hebrew Bible into Greek, so that Jews and others would have the Jewish Holy Scriptures in the Greek language. When these Hebrew scholars came to Isaiah 7:14 and the word *almah,* they translated *almah* with the Greek word *parthenos.* *Parthenos* is the definite Greek word for virgin. This Greek translation of the Hebrew Holy Scriptures by Hebrew scholars was called the Septuagint. This translation was made before Jesus was here, and the controversy over Jesus' identity had not yet arisen. The prophecy in Isaiah 7:14 definitely foretells the virgin birth of the one whom God would send to earth to die to provide the blood of atonement for believing Jews and Gentiles to be forgiven of their sins.

The one born of the virgin would be fully God, as the Messiah is, and fully human, as the son born of the virgin Jewish woman would be. The virgin birth is not a problem for God. The Almighty God of creation can do anything he desires to bring to pass his plan of salvation to lost humanity.

The Son that would be born of the virgin would be called Immanuel. Immanuel means "God with us." Because of what the Son would say and do, he would be recognized as God with us. Other prophecies that we will consider in our studies will confirm this truth.

2. *The place of his birth is foretold*

In Micah 5:2 (verse 1 in Jewish Bibles) we read, "But thou, Bethlehem Ephratah, though thou be little among the thousands of Judah, yet out of thee shall he come forth unto me that is to be ruler in Israel; whose goings forth have been from of old, from everlasting." God gives the definite location on earth where he would send his son to be born of the virgin. The address for the birth of this son is like giving someone the city, state, and country. Bethlehem would be a little town in the area of Ephratah that would be located in Judah. This is a specific location in the Holy Land.

God picked the site for the birth, his relationship to the one born and the ministry that would be accomplished. The birthplace would be Bethlehem. The child born would be of God and God's Son would someday rule Israel. This one would be of the Godhead in the Messiah, for the Messiah was from everlasting with God the Father and the Holy Spirit. The second coming of the Messiah to earth is also given here, for at that time he will defeat the enemies of Israel and rule the world from Jerusalem. How wonderful it is that we can share this prophecy with lost souls to give them a foundation for faith in Messiah Jesus.

3. *The purpose of Messiah's first coming to earth*

Isaiah chapter 53 is the greatest prophetic chapter in the Old Testament about the ministry of Messiah Jesus. Briefly stated, the fifty-third chapter of the book of

Isaiah gives to us the virgin birth, the suffering of the Messiah at the hands of unbelievers, the sinfulness of all people, the Messiah/Son's trial and his death to provide the blood of atonement for those who believe. Following his death, he is resurrected from the grave. We learn that it was the plan of God the Father to provide the blood of atonement through the death and resurrection of the Messiah/Son so that Jews and Gentiles could be forgiven of their sins.

When this chapter in the Bible has been read to Jewish people, and they were asked of whom it speaks, most said, "Jesus." After hearing that this is in the Old Testament and was written about seven hundred years before Jesus lived, Jews are shocked! Jewish people have been led to faith in Messiah Jesus as their Savior after understanding what is foretold in Isaiah 53.

4. *When will Messiah come to earth the first time?*

Daniel 9:24–27 gives us the year in which the Messiah will come to earth the first time. These verses in the book of Daniel, written about 538 bc, give us the time when the Messiah would come to earth to provide the blood of atonement for us. When these verses are understood, we know the time when Messiah would die for our sins would be about ad 32–33! Other key events in history are also foretold in this prophecy. A full study of these remarkable verses will be given in a future lesson.

THE SECOND COMING OF MESSIAH TO EARTH

The Bible clearly shows us that Messiah Jesus will come to earth the second time to bring peace to Israel and the world. These events are yet to happen in the future. Only God knows the exact time when these prophecies will be fulfilled. We do know that the second coming of Messiah Jesus will take place at the end of the great tribulation period. Let us see what God foretold through his Jewish prophets.

Zechariah 14:1–5, 14:9, 14:11 states,

> Behold, the day of the LORD cometh, and thy spoil shall be divided in the midst of thee. For I will gather all nations against Jerusalem to battle; and the city shall be taken, and the houses rifled, and the women ravished; and half of the city shall go forth into captivity, and the residue of the people shall not be cut off from the city. Then shall the LORD go forth, and fight against those nations, as when he fought in the day of battle. And his feet shall stand in that day upon the mount of Olives, which is before Jerusalem on the east, and the mount of Olives shall cleave in the midst thereof toward the east and toward the west … the LORD my God shall come, and all the saints with thee … And the LORD shall be king over all the earth: in that day shall there be one LORD, and his name one … Jerusalem shall be safely inhabited.

This prophecy, written about 487 bc, foretells the onslaught of the nations of the world against Israel and Jerusalem. When all is lost for the Jews, the LORD will come and fight against the nations and utterly defeat them by his almighty power. Notice that it says, "And his feet shall stand in that day upon the mount of Olives." Does the LORD have feet? He does here. This is none other than Messiah Jesus, for the risen Jesus has feet. Jesus showed his hands and his feet to the disciples after his resurrection as found in Luke 24:39–40.

Another truth here has personal application to all of us who are Bible-believers. When it says in these verses that the LORD comes to defeat the nations that have come against Israel and Jerusalem, it also says that all the saints come with him. True Bible-believers have been taken up to heaven, in what is called the Rapture, before the tribulation period begins on earth. In heaven, we have the judgment seat of Christ for Christians to receive our rewards and crowns for faithful service for the Lord. Then there is the marriage feast of the Lamb, a wonderful time of rejoicing! At the end of the tribulation period on earth, we will return from heaven with Messiah (Christ) Jesus when he defeats the enemies of Israel, judges the nations, and brings peace to the world. God will then begin the 1,000 years of peace on earth when believers will reign with King Jesus.

There is joy in sharing the prophecies about the two comings of the Messiah to earth. Do not hesitate to tell unsaved people about the life that can be theirs when they accept the way to be forgiven of their sins provided for them by Messiah Jesus at his first coming. As you relate what the Bible says about future events and the second coming of Messiah Jesus to earth, your witness can help Jews and Gentiles to face the future with peace and confidence as they put their faith in Jesus.

Making It Personal

1. What does Judaism teach regarding the person of the Messiah? Who is he? What is his relationship to the God of Israel?

2. What is the Jewish teaching concerning the coming of the Messiah? What will the Messiah accomplish for Israel?

3. The Bible foretells how many comings of the Messiah to earth? Give scriptural substantiation for your answer.

4. What will Messiah accomplish when he comes to earth?

5. Will understanding the comings of the Messiah to earth assist you in sharing the gospel with lost souls, especially Jewish people? Explain your answer.

6. What is the greatest prophetic chapter in the Bible about Messiah? How can you use it?

7. What verses in the Old Testament foretell the first time Messiah comes?

Additional Bible Verses for Study

- Isaiah 2
- Joel 3:9–21
- Jeremiah 23:6–8
- Psalm 110:1
- Psalm 22:1, 22:7–19
- Isaiah 9:6–8

Amazing Prophecies about Jesus

The God of Israel, through the Jewish men whom he chose (the Jewish prophets), foretold future events. In these amazing prophecies, Almighty God gave the way whereby men and women could know him and experience his forgiveness of their sins. The details given in these prophecies make it possible for Jews and Gentiles to know, beyond any doubt, who the Messiah is and his purpose in coming to earth. The coming of Messiah would open the way for a new relationship with God. Believers would possess real peace in this life and for eternity in heaven.

Learning key Old Testament prophecies about the coming of the Messiah will build and increase faith in the lives of true Christians. Seeing these prophecies fulfilled will give to all of God's people a solid foundation upon which to give an effective witness for Jesus to all lost souls.

There are two major prophecies, as well as many others, in the Old Testament about the coming of the Messiah. Knowing these prophecies is vital to an unbeliever's understanding of who the Messiah of Israel is according to the description God has given to us in his Holy Scriptures. These major prophecies are found in Isaiah 53:1–12 and Daniel 9:24–27.

Jewish people have never read these marvelous chapters in the Bible. Many Jewish Bibles have a section called the Haftorah, or Table of Scriptural Readings.

These are suggested readings for the New Year, the Sabbath, holy days and holidays, fasts, etc. The readings listed for the book of Isaiah go up to Isaiah 52:12. The next suggested reading is Isaiah 54:1–10. Isaiah 52:13–15, which are also about Messiah, and all twelve verses of chapter 53 are omitted! This does not mean that these verses are not in Jewish Bibles—they are! Since Jewish people are not instructed to read this great portion of God's Word, they have no knowledge of these Scriptures that foretell the coming of the Messiah. Daniel 9:24–27 is also not listed in the suggested readings in the Jewish Bible. These Bible verses must be shared so seeking hearts can find Jesus as their Savior.

In youth meetings that we had for many years, a Jewish teenage girl came with one of the Jewish young men. When she first came, Debbie thought it was ridiculous for a Jew to believe in Messiah Jesus. During the outings we had with the young people, we shared prophecy from the Jewish Bible. One Saturday only Debbie and Joe came. We studied Isaiah 53 verse by verse. At the conclusion of our Bible study, Debbie asked if she could take my notes home to go over them. Of course, I answered yes! When Debbie came to another meeting and returned the notes, she said, "It's all there." Another Saturday we invited a number of Jewish young people to come for a day's outing. Only Debbie and Joe came. Do not be discouraged at small numbers! That day we went over Daniel 9:24–27. Once again, Debbie asked if she could take my notes home. When she came again and returned the Daniel 9 notes, she said, "It's all there."

A short time after that, we received a telephone call about 11:00 p.m. It was Debbie. She called to tell us that she had accepted Jesus as her Messiah and Savior! The first year after she put her trust in Jesus, when she was eighteen years of age, she visited hundreds of homes and apartments in Jewish neighborhoods to share the gospel by personal testimony and giving out tracts! Giving this Jewish teenager a verse-by-verse study of Isaiah 53 and Daniel 9:24–27 brought her to place her faith in Messiah Jesus. Joe accepted Jesus as his Redeemer shortly after Debbie. Their faith in Jesus brought great joy to their lives and overflowed in sharing their new life in the Lord with countless Jews and Gentiles. They were married and have been faithfully serving the Lord for many years.

Before we study Isaiah 53 verse-by-verse, we need to look at Isaiah 52:13–15.

> Behold, my servant shall deal prudently, he shall be exalted and extolled, and be very high. As many were astonished at thee; his visage was so marred more than any man, and his form more than the sons of men: So shall he sprinkle many nations; the kings shall shut their mouths at him: for that which had not been told them shall they see; and that which they had not heard shall they consider.

The person spoken of in these verses and in chapter 52 will be God's servant. In his life, he will do the will of God and will affect nations. From a place of being exalted because of who he is, God's servant will suffer more than any man suffered. People would be astonished as they look upon this one and see the agony that he would endure.

Because of his suffering, this one would "sprinkle many nations," or people in those nations. In studying the Old Testament, we understand the meaning of the phrase "sprinkle many nations." In reading about the Day of Atonement in Leviticus 16, we know that God instructed the Jewish priest to slay the animal sacrifice and sprinkle the blood of the sacrifice upon the altar in the tabernacle. This was done so sinful people could be forgiven of their sins. Throughout the year, when a Jewish person sinned and wanted God's forgiveness, the sinner would bring the specified animal to the Jewish priest who would slay the sacrifice and " … sprinkle of the blood of the sin-offering upon the side of the altar … " which is found in Leviticus 5:6–10. When this was done, the person's sins were forgiven by God.

The one who suffers in Isaiah 52:13–15 sheds his blood for the forgiveness of the sins of the people who would accept him as their atonement. Isaiah 53 gives the details of this suffering and how sinners who accepted this one's blood sacrifice would be cleansed of sin.

These verses in Isaiah 52 also state that kings shall be put to silence when they see this one and what he does. The phrase "be exalted and extolled, and be very high" would refer to the life of this one after he dies to sprinkle many nations. He is then resurrected and ascends to the right hand of God in heaven as found in Psalm 110:1. We have in these verses, the two comings of the Messiah to earth that we have studied previously. His first coming would bring personal peace and his second coming, that is yet future, will bring world peace.

> So then faith cometh by hearing, and hearing by the Word of God.
>
> Romans 10:17

The most detailed prophecy in the Holy Scriptures concerning the first coming of the Messiah is given in Isaiah 53. This chapter has often been read to Jewish people. When these people were asked, "Of whom does this speak?"—many would respond "Jesus." Jews can be stirred to seek the truth about who Jesus is when it is shown that the fifty-third chapter of Isaiah is in the Jewish Bible and was written by the major Jewish prophet Isaiah about 700 bc!

It is important that you familiarize yourself with the twelve verses in this chapter as well as the last three verses of chapter 52. This will provide you with a foundation for sharing your faith in Jesus with a Jewish relative, friend, or contact and with Gentiles. The God of Israel, through the Jewish prophets, has given to us the basis for trusting in Jesus as our Messiah. This chapter in God's Word clearly presents the Messiah as our Redeemer who provided the blood of atonement so our sins could be forgiven. As your knowledge of these prophecies increases, you will have confidence to share your faith with all people.

Let us now consider this great prophecy in Isaiah 53 and the message God has for us to give to lost souls.

Verse 1: "Who hath believed our report? And to whom is the arm of the LORD revealed?"

These two questions will be answered in the verses that follow. The LORD will reveal himself to men and women through these verses of Holy Scripture. He will give people the opportunity to put their trust in him and his Word. God asks, "Will you believe what I am going to say to you? Will you accept what I am going to tell you about my servant, the Messiah?" The arm of the Lord can refer to the Messiah. In verses two through twelve, the LORD will reveal the purpose of the coming of Messiah in the power and strength of God, for Messiah is of the Godhead.

Verse 2: "For he shall grow up before him as a tender plant, and as a root out of a dry ground: he hath no form nor comeliness; and when we shall see him, there is no beauty that we should desire him."

The one referred to throughout this chapter will grow up before God in the will of God. The Hebrew word for dry ground in this verse is arid ground. Nothing can come out of arid ground for there is no moisture. This means that this one born into the world will come by a miraculous birth. You can also read Isaiah 7:14 when sharing verse two. The virgin birth of Messiah coming to earth to take on a human body in Jesus is clearly set forth in Isaiah 7:14.

This one has no comeliness nor beauty to attract people to himself. Of King David of Israel it was said that he was comely, or handsome. This one to come from

God would not draw people to himself because of his physical appearance. We will see in this prophecy that this one would draw people to himself by his life and what he would say and do for sinful souls. Through him, they could be forgiven of sin and be brought into a right relationship with Almighty God.

Verse 3: "He is despised and rejected of men; a man of sorrows, and acquainted with grief: and we hid as it were our faces from him; he was despised, and we esteemed him not."

The word used for the men who despised and rejected this one is the term that signifies men of stature or standing. As a whole, the leadership of Judaism would not accept this one as the Messiah. They would reject him. He would face sorrow and grief.

Verse 4: "Surely he hath borne our griefs, and carried our sorrows: yet we did esteem him stricken, smitten of God, and afflicted."

This one would bear the griefs and sorrows of suffering people. Some would interpret his burden to be an affliction from God. The Jewish people and leaders as a whole would not understand this one's mission as foretold in this fifty-third chapter of Isaiah. Messiah's first coming to earth would not bring about political deliverance from Roman oppression. The Jewish prophets, including Isaiah, did foretell that Messiah would bring peace to the Jewish people and the world; however, this world peace would come at a future time. This would happen untold years after the Messiah would come to earth the first time to bring personal peace to individuals.

Verse 5: "But he was wounded for our transgressions, he was bruised for our iniquities: the chastisement of our peace was upon him; and with his stripes we are healed."

This one would take upon himself the punishment that is due us for our sins against God. He would be wounded for our transgressions. Isaiah, who was a Hebrew or Jewish, recorded this verse of Scripture. When he refers to our transgressions and our iniquities, he speaks of the sins of the children of Israel. God's Word tells us that all people, including Gentiles, have sinned against God. In the Old Testament book of Ecclesiastes 7:20, we read, "For there is not a just man upon earth, that doeth good, and sinneth not." There are many just or good people, Jews and Gentiles, but God says that all people upon earth have sinned. In the New Testament the same truth is given in Romans 3:23, "For all have sinned, and come short of the glory of God."

The word used for wounded in this verse means mortally wounded—literally pierced unto death. This one dies so we can be forgiven of our sins. When a person commits a crime and is found guilty, he has to pay the penalty for his crime against society. When the penalty is paid, he goes free. The "chastisement of our peace was upon him" is a great truth concerning our sins and the penalty we should pay because we sin. When we put our faith in this one, and acknowledge he was put to death to take the chastisement due us for our sins, then the penalty is paid for our sins and we go free. In later studies in this book, we will consider hell and all that it means for those who die with sin in their lives. We will really understand what it means to us that our sins have been forgiven through this one who by his death and resurrection provides the blood of atonement whereby sin is forgiven.

Verse 6: "All we like sheep have gone astray; we have turned every one to his own way; and the LORD hath laid on him the iniquity of us all."

The truth that all people have sinned against God is reiterated. When a person wants his or her own way instead of God's way, it is called sin. Then the Lord tells us that he will place upon this one the sins of us all. The Bible tells us what Almighty God expects of us, such as faith in him, honesty, purity, clean language, no idolatry, no lying, no adultery, no stealing, and many other laws that are given to us by God who created us. However, people do not obey all of God's laws and they sin against God. When our sins are forgiven and we live for God, our lives are filled with joy, peace, and contentment. There is no fear of death because we know we are going to heaven when we die. The blessings that God gives to people who trust him cannot be numbered!

Why then do Jews and Gentiles not believe in God and Messiah Jesus? It is sad to say that many people have seen hypocrisy in the lives of some professing Christians. This has turned them away from seeking and trusting God, Christ Jesus, and the Bible. You and I must live godly lives before the unsaved and share the gospel with them! Many will be saved if we give them the opportunity to know the truth. Let us be faithful to the Lord and give the gospel to lost souls.

Verse 7: "He was oppressed, and he was afflicted, yet he opened not his mouth: he is brought as a lamb to the slaughter, and as a sheep before her shearers is dumb, so he openeth not his mouth."

This verse reveals to us that this one will be brought to a trial where he would not speak to defend himself against his accusers. He would be brought as a sacrificial lamb to be put to death. When a sheep is sheared, it remains quiet. So also it will be with this one when people speak against him.

Verse 8: "He was taken from prison and from judgment: and who shall declare his generation? For he was cut off out of the land of the living: for the transgression of my people was he stricken."

The prophecy speaks of this one being taken from prison and from a trial. "Who shall declare his generation" could mean that at the trial no one would speak on his behalf. This could also refer to all people who would believe in him for the cleansing of their sins that they should tell others about him. The conclusion of the trial and events that followed culminated in the death of this one. The verse clearly says he was cut off out of the land of the living. This is death. This is in the past tense, for Isaiah saw this future event happen and recorded it as having been done. In prophecy, events that are future can be recorded as having happened, but are still future. As previously mentioned, Isaiah recorded this prophecy about seven hundred years before Christ, but the events that God revealed to him were so vivid that he wrote as if they had happened. The purpose of God in this one's death cannot be clearer. He dies so that transgressors, or sinners, could be forgiven of their sins.

Verse 9: "And he made his grave with the wicked, and with the rich in his death; because he had done no violence, neither was any deceit in his mouth."

What a marvelous prophecy! After this one dies, he should have been buried with sinners, or the wicked. This was the plan of those who put him to death. Then a rich person would intervene, because he knew that the one put to death was not a sinner or wicked person. This one had done no violence, neither was any deceit in his mouth. This cannot be said of any human being for we all have sinned. This one had no sin in him. This prophecy is very specific. This one would be buried in a rich man's tomb!

Verse 10: "Yet it pleased the LORD to bruise him; he hath put him to grief: when thou shalt make his soul an offering for sin, he shall see his seed, he shall prolong his days, and the pleasure of the LORD shall prosper in his hand."

There is much truth in this verse. Many questions are answered. Who is responsible for the death of Jesus? The Jews have been blamed for it for years. This Scripture says, "Yet it pleased the LORD to bruise him;

he [God]…made his [this one's] soul an offering for sin." Almighty God planned the death of this one to provide the blood of atonement offering needed for us to be forgiven of our sins. All people are responsible for the death of this one for we all have sinned. He died for us so we could be cleansed of our sins. Then the resurrection of this one from the grave, and his future ministry, are foretold. After his death and burial, "He shall see his seed, he shall prolong his days, and the pleasure of the LORD shall prosper in his hand." A dead person does not see his seed—in this case spiritual seed or people who have had their sins forgiven by this one's atonement for them. "He shall prolong his days" means the LORD will give resurrection life to his servant who had died. Then the pleasure of the LORD shall prosper in his hand. The pleasure of God would not prosper in the life of a dead person. This one is alive and has a ministry for the Godhead in the hearts of Jews and Gentiles who will put their trust in him. We know from this prophecy and history that the one spoken of in Isaiah 53 is Messiah Jesus.

Verse 11: "He shall see of the travail of his soul, and shall be satisfied: by his knowledge shall my righteous servant justify many; for he shall bear their iniquities."

Blessing from Almighty God comes to believers. God will see what this one has done when he died for us to be forgiven of our sins. God is satisfied with his blood offering for our atonement and cleansing. The believer in this one, Messiah Jesus, has the assurance that all sin has been forgiven. Messiah Jesus paid the debt in full for us to be made right with God. Peace is a reality for this life and for eternity! There is no sin in God or in heaven. When our sins have been forgiven by God, a place in heaven has been reserved for us for eternity!

This verse also contains a warning to all people who are yet unbelievers. "By his knowledge [or by knowing him, believing in Messiah Jesus] shall my righteous servant justify many." The blood of Jesus will make atonement for every believer, but Jews and Gentiles, men, women, and young people must put their trust in him. The verse says he will justify many, not everyone. Only those who put their faith in God's plan for their lives through Messiah Jesus will be forgiven of their sins.

Verse 12: "Therefore will I divide him a portion with the great, and he shall divide the spoil with the strong; because he hath poured out his soul unto death: and he was numbered with the transgressors; and he bare the sin of many, and made intersession for the transgressors."

Truth already given in the previous verses is reiterated. Jesus dies to provide the blood of atonement for us to be forgiven of our sins. Only believers in God and Messiah Jesus and God's plan for the forgiveness of sin will be made right with God. Messiah Jesus would pray for the sinners who put him to death on the tree.

In the additional Bible verses for study section, you will find New Testament verses that show Jesus fulfilled every prophecy given in Isaiah 53. Praise the Lord!

Before we close this section of our study, we will

share with you Judaism's interpretation of Isaiah 53. This is important as new Jewish believers, especially young people, are often taken by their parents to a rabbi to have the rabbi talk them out of their faith in Messiah Jesus. Since Isaiah 53 is in the Jewish Holy Scriptures, it is difficult for a rabbi to dispute. One example is Abe Sandler who was saved in our youth ministry. When his Orthodox Jewish parents heard of his faith in Jesus, they insisted that Abe visit the family's rabbi so he could talk their son into renouncing Jesus. We prayed with Abe for victory for him at his meeting with the rabbi. During his visit, Abe shared his testimony and why he believed in Jesus. He told the rabbi about Isaiah 53 and other Old Testament prophecies about Messiah that have been fulfilled in Jesus. At the conclusion of their conversation, the rabbi did not refute Abe's experience and his new life in Messiah, but he sent him to another rabbi. The same result happened with the second rabbi! Abe knew what he believed and why, and no one was going to talk him out of his faith in the Lord. He knew how to share Isaiah 53 and to refute the Jewish arguments against Jesus. The second rabbi sent Abe to a liberal Gentile minister who, after hearing Abe share his faith and respond to questions, said, "Keep up the good work." Many rabbis will be unmoved by a Jewish believer's experience and testimony about Messiah Jesus and will endeavor to turn the believer away from Jesus and back to Judaism. Much prayer, love and guidance will sustain the new believers and see them through persecution, stress and enticements.

Most rabbis will say that Isaiah 53 does not speak of the Messiah and not of Jesus. The Jewish inquirer will be told that the Jewish interpretation of the "he" in the twelve verses refers to the nation of Israel or the Jewish people. The rabbi will not give any further information and will expect his simple statement to be accepted as fact. In the past, many older rabbis who wrote about Isaiah 53 said that the "he" of this chapter is the Messiah. Today, Judaism teaches that Isaiah 53 describes the people of Israel and their suffering.

The reasons why we know Isaiah 53 speaks of Messiah Jesus are:

Verse 2	The one spoken of would not be comely and have no beauty or physical attractiveness. This is not true of many Jewish people.
Verse 4	Though Jewish people have suffered much, it was not that they were bearing the sorrows and grief of other people.
Verse 6	God did not lay the sins of all people on the Jews so people could be forgiven of their sins. It says in Psalm 49:6–8, "They that trust in their wealth, and boast themselves in the multitude of their riches; None of them can by any means redeem his brother, nor give to God a ransom for him (for the redemption of their soul is precious, and it ceaseth

forever)." A person cannot redeem another lost soul.

Verse 7	This says that when this one would suffer, he would not fight back. The nation of Israel has and always should defend herself.
Verse 8	He was cut off out of the land of the living. This would mean that all Jews would die. Another prophecy that we will study tells us that Messiah would die about ad 32–33. If the one in Isaiah 53 is Israel or the Jewish people, then there would be no Israel or Jewish people living today.
Verse 9	This one dies, but it is said of him that he never sinned. This cannot be said of any person or nation.
Verses 10–12	God would never make any human being or nation an offering for sin so sinners could be forgiven.

Making It Personal

1. How do we explain prophecy in the Old Testament? What is it?

2. Why should we use prophecies when sharing the gospel?

3. What are the two major prophecies about the coming of Messiah in the Jewish Bible? Can sharing these prophecies actually lead a Jewish person to faith in Jesus? Practice sharing these prophecies with someone in your group or a friend.

4. What key Scripture verses precede Isaiah 53? What do these verses tell us?

5. Explain briefly how you can share Isaiah 53.

6. How do rabbis and Judaism interpret Isaiah 53 and how can you refute it?

Additional Bible Verses for Study

- Isaiah 53:1   John 12:36–38, Romans 10:16
- Isaiah 53:2   Luke 1:26–45, Matthew 1:18–25
- ISAIAH 53:3   Matthew 27:1–2, 27:30–31
- Isaiah 53:4   Matthew 8:16–17, 1 Peter 2:24
- Isaiah 53:5   John 1:29, 11:49–52, Acts 10:43
- Isaiah 53:6   Romans 3:23, 5:8–11, 6:23
- Isaiah 53:7   Matthew 26:62–64, Mark 15:1–3
- ISAIAH 53:8   Matthew 27:35–50, Luke 23:1–25, PSALM 22:18
- Isaiah 53:9   Matthew 27:57–60
- Isaiah 53:10   Psalm 16:9–10, Psalm 110:1, Matthew 28:1–10

- Isaiah 53:11   Acts 2:22–32, 13:38–39, Colossians 1:12–14, John 3:16
- Isaiah 53:12   Romans 3:25, Mark 15:27–28, Luke 23:32–34

When Will Messiah Come?

The early church was given instructions to spread the gospel to all nations. The first people to hear God's plan of salvation were Jews in the land of Israel. After the Jewish people in Jerusalem and the Holy Land heard the good news of salvation in Messiah Jesus, the believers were to reach unsaved souls among the Jews as well as the Gentiles. God has never changed this order of evangelism. The Lord through the Apostle Paul wrote in Romans 1:16, "For I am not ashamed of the gospel of Christ: for it is the power of God unto salvation to every one that believeth; to the Jew first, and also to the Greek [Gentile]." In his journeys to share the gospel, Paul went to speak to Jews in the synagogue first and then he turned to the Gentiles in that community. This burden upon the heart of the Apostle Paul for his Jewish people to know Messiah Jesus should rest upon us today. It is God's desire that we, who are his children through Christ Jesus, share the gospel with the children of Israel and the Gentiles.

> And that repentance and remission of sins should be preached in his name among all nations, beginning at Jerusalem.
>
> Luke 24:47

We read in Romans 10:17, "So then faith cometh by hearing, and hearing by the Word of God." As Jews and Gentiles hear the Word of God—the gospel—they will have the foundation upon which faith is built, but they must hear! Then they will be able to believe. Fulfilled prophecy is one of the keys that will lead seeking hearts to trust in Jesus. In our last lesson we learned how the fifty-third chapter of Isaiah foretells the birth, life, death, and resurrection of the Jewish Messiah. This detailed prophecy, written about 700 bc, was totally fulfilled in the life of Jesus.

Do we have God-given Scripture that foretold just when all this would come to pass? Can we find the time in history when the Messiah would come to provide the blood of atonement for Jews and Gentiles to be forgiven of their sins?

Yes, we can! The second greatest prophecy in the Old Testament was recorded about 538 bc and is found in Daniel 9:24–27. The twelve verses in Isaiah 53 are such a marvelous, wonderful prophecy about Jesus. Likewise, these four verses in Daniel 9 are tremendous. In this prophecy, we have the time when Messiah Jesus would be here on earth. Most Jewish people have never heard this great prophecy. Many Christians also have never studied these verses in Daniel 9. Your faith will be increased as you understand this prophecy. Your knowledge of how to share the gospel will be grounded in new facts that will be a blessing to you and to those to whom you witness.

The background information you should know before sharing this prophecy is found in Daniel 9:1–23.

Read these verses so that you are familiar with them. The basic truths presented are:

Verse 1 — Daniel was a Jewish captive in Babylon under King Darius.

Verse 2 — Daniel knew from the prophecy and book written by Jeremiah that the Jewish captivity would last for seventy years. The captivity was almost over and Jerusalem was in ruins.

Verses 3–16 — Daniel confessed to God the sins of his Jewish people.

Verses 17–19 — Daniel prays for Jerusalem and the temple to be restored and the Jewish people to return to the land of Israel.

Verses 20–23 — The angel Gabriel is sent from God to give Daniel wisdom and understanding concerning future events.

> Ye are the light of the world … Neither do men light a candle and put it under a bushel, but on a candlestick … Let your light so shine before men, that they may see your good works, and glorify your Father which is in heaven.
>
> Matthew 5:14–16

Let us consider the prophecy verse by verse.

Verse 24: "Seventy weeks are determined upon thy people and upon thy holy city, to finish the transgression, and to make an end of sins, and to make reconciliation for iniquity, and to bring in everlasting righteousness, and to seal up the vision and prophecy, and to anoint the most Holy."

The word weeks in the original Hebrew is *shavu'im.* It is plural and can mean seven-year periods. As we consider this amazing prophecy in these verses and in Daniel 12:11–12, it will be seen that *shavu'im* here definitely means periods of seven years and not weeks of seven days. As we read, every time that the word weeks appears, it should be sevens. We will see that the prophecy speaks of years.

The prophecy will affect "thy people," who are Daniel's Jewish people, and "thy holy city," which is Jerusalem. At the end of the last seven years of the prophecy, there will be world peace that God himself will bring to the earth. At this time, Almighty God will make an end of sins and, by his power, bring righteousness to the world. There will be no more prophecy for it will not be needed. God will anoint the Most Holy. This will be the place upon earth from where God the Messiah will rule the world. Much detail of what will happen is given in Isaiah, Zechariah, and other books in the Old Testament, as well as in the books of the New Testament, especially Revelation.

Verse 25: "Know therefore and understand, that from the going forth of the commandment to restore and to build

Jerusalem unto the Messiah the Prince shall be seven weeks [sevens], and threescore and two weeks [sevens]: the street shall be built again, and the wall, even in troublous times."

When this prophecy was given to Daniel, Jerusalem and the wall about the city were in ruins. A ruler would give a commandment, or authority, for someone to go to Jerusalem to rebuild the city. This authority would include the wall about Jerusalem. In those days, a wall was needed to protect a city. The beginning of the seventy sevens would be the date in history that a ruler would give this commandment to rebuild Jerusalem and the wall about it.

When the beginning date would be established, we count off seven sevens, 7 x 7, or 49. Then we count off threescore and two (sixty-two) sevens, or 62 x 7 which is 434. Add the two figures of 49 and 434 together, and we have 483. When you share this prophecy, it would help the inquirer if you have pencil and paper to draw a time line to show how these years add up. Later in this study, we will prove from the book of Daniel that this period of time refers to years.

What will happen after 483 years following the commandment to rebuild Jerusalem? Messiah the Prince will be here on earth! God tells us in this prophecy just when the Messiah would come to this world! This would be Messiah's first coming to earth.

Notice the first forty-nine years are separated from the remaining 434 years. The early years of the first period of time, 7 x 7, would include the rebuilding of the wall about Jerusalem and other construction in the city. Verse 25 also tells us that Jerusalem and the wall would be rebuilt in troublous times. There would be opposition to the rebuilding. When we read the book of Nehemiah and his task to rebuild the wall and Jerusalem, we learn about the opposition he and the Jewish people faced from enemies who did not want the wall to be rebuilt. When did this happen? What is the beginning date of these events in this prophecy?

In the Old Testament book of Nehemiah, we have the writing of this Jewish man of God. In chapter 1, we learn that Jerusalem and the wall were in ruins. Nehemiah is burdened for his Jewish people and is led by God to ask King Artaxerxes, for whom he was the cupbearer, to help him go to Jerusalem to rebuild (Nehemiah 2:1–8). King Artaxerxes gave the commandment for Nehemiah to return to Jerusalem to rebuild the wall and the city. The king also provided provisions and building materials for Nehemiah as well as soldiers to protect him on the journey to Jerusalem. God works in the hearts of world rulers to bring to pass his will!

The commandment to rebuild was given to Nehemiah in the twentieth year of King Artaxerxes' reign. This was the year 445 bc. It was in the month Nisan, which is April (Nehemiah 2:1). This marvelous prophecy about the Messiah and other events begins with the year 445 bc.

Verse 26: "And after threescore and two weeks [sevens] shall Messiah be cut off, but not for himself: and the people of the prince that shall come shall destroy the

George and Jean Gruen

city and the sanctuary; and the end thereof shall be with a flood, and unto the end of the war desolations are determined."

The prophecy continues with the solemn words of what happens to the Messiah after the period of 434 years that follows the forty-nine years. After the total of 483 years, the Messiah would be cut off.

Do you remember seeing the words cut off in our study of Isaiah 53? In the prophecy of Isaiah 53:8–10 and 53:12,

> He was taken from prison and from judgment: and who shall declare his generation? For he was cut off out of the land of the living: for the transgression of my people was he stricken. And he made his grave with the wicked, and with the rich in his death; because he had done no violence, neither was any deceit in his mouth. Yet it pleased the LORD to bruise him … when thou shalt make his soul an offering for sin … because he hath poured out his soul unto death … and he bare the sin of many …

The Messiah, whom we know from all of the prophecies, is Jesus. Messiah Jesus would suffer death in our place to take the punishment due us for our sins. We have God's forgiveness of our sins when we trust in Jesus. He does not die for himself, for he is sinless. He is cut off, or dies, for us. Many will accept the blood of atonement provided for us by Messiah Jesus, but not all people will believe God's plan of salvation.

Daniel's prophecy continues in verse 26. After Messiah is cut-off or dies, another prince would come with people who will destroy the city and the sanctuary. The city is Jerusalem and the sanctuary is the Jewish temple in Jerusalem. The city of Jerusalem and the temple were destroyed by the Roman army in a d 70. This is well documented in history. This destruction was like a flood with great desolation. This terrible massacre of Jewish people and the destruction of Jerusalem and the temple will never be forgotten.

According to the Holy Scriptures in Daniel 9, the Messiah would die before this awful destruction by the Roman army in a d 70. Jesus' death for our sins did happen before the unbelievable events that came upon the Jewish people and Jerusalem in a d 70. Messiah Jesus died about a d 32–33. When using 360 days in a year of the Jewish calendar, the time when Messiah would be cut off comes out to when Jesus died. God's Word is true and what he foretells will come to pass!

> And they that be wise shall shine as the brightness of the firmament; and they that turn many to righteousness as the stars for ever and ever.
>
> Daniel 12:3

Verse 27: "And he shall confirm the covenant with many for one week [seven]: and in the midst of the week [seven] he shall cause the sacrifice and the oblation to cease, and for the over-spreading of abominations he shall make it desolate, even until the consummation, and that determined shall be poured upon the desolate."

There is an undetermined passing of time between the events in verse 26 and verse 27. This is not stated, but events and other Scriptures confirm this truth. We are living in this gap period that will continue until we see events in the world shaping up for the fulfillment of the prophecy in this verse in the Holy Bible. We will not include in this study the events that will occur in the coming of Christ Jesus in the clouds for believers in the Rapture (1 Thessalonians 4:13–18 and other Scriptures). The coming of the Lord in the air to take us up to heaven can happen at any time, but the day that this will be a reality is known only to God. After the Rapture, the prophecy of verse 27 will be fulfilled. No date is given as to when this seven-year period will begin; however, some of the events that precede it are seen today.

Verse 27 states that another world ruler will arise who will make a covenant with the Jewish people to permit them to worship in their rebuilt temple. This ruler will grant the Jewish people a period of seven years (the last seven in the prophecy in Daniel 9:27) to worship in the temple. In the midst (the Hebrew word means in the middle) of the seven years, this ruler will break his covenant with Israel and cause the temple worship and sacrifices to cease. For three and a half years, the Jewish people will worship in their rebuilt temple. Then this anti-god ruler will turn against them, take control of the temple and pollute it. Following this, there will be great suffering and desolation in the world as we read in the book of Revelation. God's judgments will come upon the earth.

There are very important things to consider here. The nations will have to see a world ruler come to power. The Jewish temple will have to be rebuilt so the world ruler can make a covenant with the Jewish people for them to worship there for seven years. When Christians begin to see these things happen, we are told to look for the return of Messiah Jesus to take true Bible-believers out of this world. We are to be ready for the Lord's return. We believe that there are Jewish people and Gentiles to whom we witness now, who do not accept Jesus as their Savior, who will be among the tribulation saints spoken of in the book of Revelation. Let us be faithful in sharing the gospel at every opportunity the Lord gives to us.

YEARS VS. DAYS

There is one question that must be answered for us to know the timing involved in this great prophecy given through Daniel to the Jewish people and the world. How can we know that this entire prophecy deals with years? The verses in Daniel 12:1–12 give us the answer. In particular, Daniel 12:8–12,

> And I [Daniel] heard, but I understood not: then said I, O my LORD, what shall be the end of these things? And he said, Go thy way, Daniel: for the words are closed up and sealed till the time of the end. Many shall be purified, and made white,

George and Jean Gruen

and tried; but the wicked shall do wickedly: and none of the wicked shall understand; but the wise shall understand. And from the time that the daily sacrifice shall be taken away, and the abomination that maketh desolate set up, there shall be a thousand two hundred and ninety days. Blessed is he that waiteth, and cometh to the thousand three hundred and five and thirty days.

What do these verses tell us? From the time that the daily sacrifice in the Jewish temple is stopped and the temple is polluted, there will follow 1,290 days. This is a little over three and a half years. The temple worship is ended in the middle of the last seven. From the middle until the end is three and a half years; therefore, the seven is seven years and all of the sevens are periods of years. As mentioned before, the Hebrew word in your Bible that is translated "weeks" is also translated multiples of seven years which is the correct translation in these verses in Daniel 9:24–27.

Then Daniel 12:12 gives a period of forty-five days longer than the three and a half years. The people that live through those added days are blessed. Much death and desolation will happen upon the earth in the days after the temple is polluted. Almighty God pours out judgment upon the world as he has revealed in the book of Revelation and other Old Testament and New Testament Scriptures. The people who live through this great judgment with its desolation, destruction and death will be blessed because they are still alive. They will have seen Messiah Jesus return at the end of the tribulation and defeat the armies of the world that have come against Jerusalem. History has recorded the fulfillments of these great prophecies given in Daniel 9:25–26. The events in Daniel 9:24 and 9:27 might not be far off. Let us keep our eyes on Jesus and serve the Lord now by spreading the gospel to lost Jews and Gentiles while we yet have time!

Making It Personal

1. What do we learn from Daniel 9:25–26 about Messiah? Did Jesus fulfill these prophecies? What other main prophecy in Isaiah should you use with these verses in Daniel 9?

2. When was this prophecy recorded? Is this a useful tool to share God's word with the unsaved? Why?

3. Who were Nehemiah and King Artaxerxes? How do they enter this prophecy?

4. What future events are foretold in Daniel 9:24–27? How should these events influence our living today?

5. Do you have a clear understanding of what Daniel 9:24–27 foretells and can you use it to witness for the Lord?

6. Does human history confirm the accuracy of Bible prophecy?

Additional Bible Verses for Study

- Nehemiah 1, 2, 4:1–6, 6:15–16
- Zechariah 14:1–9
- Revelation 5 and 8
- Revelation 6:9–17
- Revelation 11:1–3
- Revelation 15:1–4

The Bible

PART A
You Can Trust the Bible—God's Word

Except for Orthodox Jews, and perhaps Conservatives, the average Jewish person you will meet has little or no faith in God. They are agnostics or atheists. To them, the Bible is a book with some truth but is made up of many stories that are fables, fairy tales, and the imagination of people. Jews have seen much hypocrisy in the lives of many people who profess to be Christians. These Gentiles, who consider themselves to be Christians, occasionally attend a church service and say they believe in God; however, they do not live according to what the Bible teaches. Anti-Semitism, with its many avenues of persecution of Jewish people, is still prevalent throughout the world. Since many Jews believe that if you are not Jewish you are a Christian, we can understand their unbelief and rejection of the Bible. These dear Jewish people are lost souls. The inner spiritual void is causing some to seek the truth about God and eternity. Their disillusionment with organized religion can be resolved by the intelligent presentation of God's Word from a Spirit-led, loving, Bible-believer who shares a personal walk with God through Messiah Jesus. We do not present a religion but a wonderful relationship with the God of Israel for this life and life after death.

In this study, we will consider how you can present the Bible to a Jew or Gentile in a way that can lead them to faith in God, Messiah Jesus, and the Bible. In all of your contacts, remember what the Apostle Paul did as he approached lost souls with the gospel as recorded for us in Romans 10:1–4,

> Brethren, my heart's desire and prayer to God for Israel is, that they might be saved. For I bear them record that they have a zeal of God, but not according to knowledge. For they being ignorant of God's righteousness, and going about to establish their own righteousness, have not submitted themselves unto the righteousness of God. For Christ is the end of the law for righteousness to every one that believeth.

We must have a heart burden for lost souls. This burden is to be followed by earnest prayer that the person with a seeking heart will listen to our testimony. Ask your Christian friends to pray with you for the salvation of your contact. We also need to understand that unsaved Jews and Gentiles will have some form of good works or deeds that they believe will please God. In our witness, we must share the prophecies about Messiah Jesus that can lead seeking souls to faith and salvation.

A foundation for faith is essential in leading a lost soul to the Lord. In our witness to Jewish people and

Gentiles, we use the following three basic truths to answer the question, "How do you know the Bible is true?"

1. INTERNAL EVIDENCE

Fulfilled prophecy proves that Almighty God gave us the Bible. The future events that were foretold through the Jewish prophets in the Old Testament were recorded hundreds of years before the events transpired. No man or woman could have anticipated them. The fact that all Bible prophecies that should have been fulfilled to date have come to pass show us that the Bible is the Word of God and is trustworthy.

There is one great theme throughout the Holy Scriptures—redemption. Men and women sin against God. God planned the way for sinful people to be forgiven of their sins. This plan of God is found in the pages of the Bible. It is revealed in the many prophecies and the fulfillments that God gave throughout the Holy Scriptures. The LORD used about forty authors to give us the Bible over a period of about 1,600 years. There are thirty-nine books in the Jewish Bible (Old Testament) and twenty-seven in the New Testament. God's plan for men and women is made clear in the combined study of the books of the Bible. No other writing, philosophy, or teaching will bring to human hearts the reality of peace in this life and for eternity in heaven. This great assurance is real in the lives of those who put their faith in what the Bible teaches us.

> So then faith cometh by hearing, and hearing by the Word of God.
>
> Romans 10:17

The fulfilled prophecies in God's Word will bring faith to the seeking heart. In our studies, we have shared a number of key prophecies given by God through the Jewish men that he chose to write the Bible. Be certain to share Isaiah 53, Micah 5:2, Isaiah 7:14, Isaiah 48:16–17, Daniel 9:24–27, Jeremiah 23:4–6, Isaiah 9:6, and Psalm 110:1.

Read these prophecies slowly to your friend and explain them. Ask the one with whom you are sharing God's Word to give his or her understanding of what the prophecies say concerning the Messiah. All of these Scriptures foretell the coming of the Messiah and clearly reveal that Jesus is the one who fulfilled them. He is the Messiah and our Redeemer from sin.

When sharing with a Jewish person of the Orthodox or Conservative faith, be certain to explain that Bible prophecies make it clear that the Messiah comes to earth two times. His first coming is to provide the blood of atonement for us to be forgiven of our sins—personal peace. After his death, resurrection, and ascension to the right hand of God, Messiah Jesus will yet come in the future to defeat the enemies of Israel and bring peace to Jerusalem and to all Jews and Gentiles—world peace. Read Isaiah 2:1–5 and Zechariah 14:1–9, 14:11. Verse 9 of Zechariah 14 reads, "And the LORD shall be king over all the earth: in that day shall there be one LORD, and his name one." In our study of Deuteronomy 6:4, we saw that God is one and that the word for one is *echad*, which can mean a unity, or more than one. Jewish teaching is that God is only one and that Messiah Jesus cannot be God. We know from the Old Testament that *echad* is a unity as in husband and wife in Genesis 2:24. Here in Zechariah 14:9 the Hebrew word for one is also "*echad*." As we consider the Bible verses concerning the Godhead and the Messiah, we know that the "one" in this verse in Zechariah speaks of the Godhead, God the Father, God the Messiah, and God the Holy Spirit, ruling over the earth.

2. EXTERNAL EVIDENCE

Can we show that the Bible is the Word of God because it always gives us the truth in all that is written? Yes! This is evident from outside sources that confirm the Biblical record is accurate and can be trusted. The external evidence is provided by the findings of archaeologists. Archaeologists have explored many mounds or "tells" that have given us facts about history that happened thousands of years ago. A "tell" in the Middle East is a large mound or hill that was built up over the years when the remains of successive communities or cities were destroyed and buried. Each community had a definite, distinct, stratum of its own, containing implements, pottery, rubbish, records, and relics of the people. When an invading army captured a city, the victors would not live in the buildings they had captured. The buildings and houses would be leveled with the relics, artifacts, and names. A new city would be built upon the old one that had been destroyed. There are some mounds or "tells" that are over a hundred feet high and contain as many as twenty or more leveled cities. Archaeologists have dug down through the remains of these cities and uncovered amazing facts.

In Isaiah 20:1 we read, "In the year that Tartan came to Ashdod (when Sargon the king of Assyria sent him), and fought against Ashdod, and took it." Another reference in 2 Kings 18:17 mentions the king of Assyria (but not his name) sending Tartan and a great army against Jerusalem at another time. People who do not believe you can trust the Bible said that when King Sargon was named in Isaiah 20:1, the writers of the Bible made a great error. They said that King Sargon was never mentioned in secular history and that he did not exist; therefore, no one should accept the Biblical records.

In the mid 1800s, an archeologist by the name of Paul Botta discovered the ruins of King Sargon's palace in Khorsabad on the north edge of Ninevah with treasures, inscriptions and his name. King Sargon was one of Assyria's greatest kings. The Bible is correct and true to history. The critics of the Bible were wrong.

Non-believers of God's Word said that the Bible was in error when Edom was mentioned during the eras of King David and King Solomon. In 2002, an archeological dig in Jordan substantiated the mention of Edom in the Holy Scriptures. The critics of the Bible were wrong, as they are in every case. God's Word is always true and reliable. We can put our trust in all that God has said to us in the Bible. The peace, joy, guidance, victory, and blessings of Almighty God, through Messiah Jesus, given in the Bible, are ours today and will be forever in heaven. Your local Bible bookstore will have good books on archaeology that will be a blessing to you and to others through you.

3. PERSONAL EVIDENCE

In Psalm 34:8, it states, "O taste and see that the LORD is good: blessed is the man that trusteth in him." When we put our trust in God's plan for our lives, we will never be disappointed! Knowing the Lord these many years has brought us through many trials, difficult times, and hardship. Through them all, the peace of God in Christ Jesus has supported us and given the ability to press on. There have always been verses in the Bible that have sustained us and given victory. In the midst of tears, there is peace when God is in control of our lives.

In October 2001, George's wife Doris died and left this life for her new home in heaven. She had been ill for sometime. She was now free from pain and death. George and Doris had been married for fifty-one years and one month when she was called to heaven. In Revelation 21:4, we have this promise from the Lord, "And God shall wipe away all tears from their eyes; and there shall be no more death, neither sorrow, nor crying, neither shall there be any more pain: for the former things are passed away."

In September 1996, Jean's husband Richard died at age fifty after a one-year battle with leukemia. He, too, was now free from the pain and suffering of this world. They had been married twenty-nine years and one week. At his funeral service, Jean could sing with conviction beautiful and meaningful hymns because she knew that Christ Jesus had paid the price for eternal life. How did she know? Jean knew because she read it in the Bible and she knew the Bible is true.

George and Jean could each stand at the gravesites of their beloved spouses and know they have new life and are safe forever with the Lord in heaven.

> Blessed be the God and Father of our Lord Jesus Christ, which according to his abundant mercy hath begotten us again unto a lively hope by the resurrection of Jesus Christ from the dead, to an inheritance incorruptible, and undefiled, and that fadeth not away, reserved in heaven for you.
>
> 1 Peter 1:3–4

People will say they are not afraid to die. They believe death ends it all. When we talk with these lost souls, we share our experiences of seeing Doris and Rich leave this life through the doorway of death to enter the Lord's presence in heaven. We also say to them, "You are not dying now. I would like to talk with you when the doctor tells you that you have a week or a month to live."

In sharing the gospel with unsaved people, ask them to consider the following: "I am a Bible-believer and have faith that the Bible is true. According to what God has promised in the Bible, I know that when I die I will go to heaven for eternity where there will be peace and joy forever. If the Bible is not true, when I die there will be nothing after death. I will have lived a good life, but death will end it all. In either situation, I cannot lose. You do not believe the Bible is true. You believe that when you die, death will end it all. Whatever life you have lived, it will end at death. This will be true, if what the Bible teaches is not true. If the Bible is true, when you die you will go to an eternal hell of darkness, suffering, and sorrow forever. Because I trust God, I cannot lose. You do not trust God. By your unbelief you can lose. The Bible says there is no second chance to believe after you die. Isn't it worth it for you today to look into what the Bible teaches?"

> And many of them that sleep in the dust of the earth shall awake, some to everlasting life, and some to shame and everlasting contempt. And they that be wise shall shine as the brightness of the firmament; and they that turn many to righteousness as the stars for ever and ever.
>
> Daniel 12:2–3

Dear brethren, be faithful in sharing your faith in God, Christ Jesus, and the Bible. We can trust the Holy Scriptures completely, for it is the Word of Almighty God to our hearts. Unsaved souls must be told the gospel, and many will only hear it if we tell them.

PART B
Understanding the Jewish Bible

The Jewish Bible that is used by Orthodox and Conservative Jewish people, as well as other Jews, will be different from your Bible. The order of the thirty-nine books in the Jewish Bible is set up according to sections. If a Jewish person wants you to read from the Bible in his or her possession, the following information will be important. Another name for their Bible is the *Tenach*.

The following is the order of the thirty-nine books in the Jewish Bible:

First Section: The Pentateuch or the Law

Genesis, Exodus, Leviticus, Numbers, and Deuteronomy. These five books are known as the Torah, or the five books of Moses. They are held in high esteem and will be accepted when, at times, other books in the Jewish Bible are not. These books are the same order as your Bible. The books that follow are in a different order.

Second Section: The Earlier Prophets

Joshua, Judges, 1 Samuel, 2 Samuel, 1 Kings, and 2 Kings.

Third Section:	The Later Prophets
	Isaiah, Jeremiah, Ezekiel, Hosea, Joel, Amos, Obadiah, Jonah, Micah, Nahum, Habakkuk, Zephaniah, Haggai, Zechariah, and Malachi.
Fourth Section:	The Holy Writings
	Psalms, Proverbs, Job, Song of Songs (or Solomon), Ruth, Lamentations, Ecclesiastes, Esther, Daniel, Ezra, Nehemiah, 1 Chronicles, and 2 Chronicles.

Jewish Bibles often read from the back to the front. Do not be surprised if you have to turn to what would be the back cover to begin! From there you will have to look for the different sections and then the book in that section.

The translation of the Hebrew into English might also be different than your Bible. Usually the truth presented is the same, except for the prophecies about the Messiah. In Isaiah 9:6 our Bible reads, "For unto us a child is born, unto us a son is given: and the government shall be upon his shoulder: and his name shall be called Wonderful, Counselor, The mighty God, The everlasting Father, The Prince of Peace." This is a correct translation of the Hebrew with the commas placed as they should be. This prophecy tells us that the Son born will be called the names of Almighty God. This prophecy, combined with many others, tells us that Messiah Jesus is one in the Godhead.

Jewish translations have changed this verse in

Isaiah 9. Instead of it being verse 6, they make it verse 5. The 1916 Hebrew Publishing Company's Alexander Harkavy translation reads, "…and his name shall be called Wonderful, Counselor of the Mighty God, of the Everlasting Father, Prince of Peace." The Hebrew text does not have "of the" in it. This older translation by Harkavy conformed to the teaching of Judaism that Jews are not to believe Jesus is the Messiah. This older translation is no longer in print. Newer Jewish translations conform to the same teaching that is prevalent in synagogues and Jewish places of worship that Messiah is not God.

True Bible-believing Christians must share the prophecies about Jesus. Without our witness, lost souls will never know God's truth about Messiah and salvation in Jesus. Many Christians believe that Jews know a great deal about the Old Testament. Since most Christians' knowledge of the Jewish Bible is minimal, they hesitate to witness. They feel they will make a mistake and hinder Jews from being saved. Except for many Orthodox Jews, Jewish people as a whole know virtually nothing about what their Bible teaches. They probably know something about other Jewish books, such as the *Siddur* or prayer book, but their knowledge of God's Word is nil.

As you share the gospel with Jews, you will find many are atheists or agnostics. They have been disillusioned with the Jewish faith, for it has not met their spiritual need. As a result, they have also turned away from God and the Holy Scriptures. Anti-Semitism has caused many Jews to feel that Gentiles and even Christians hate them. They do not know where to turn to find real peace.

A Jewish man, after trying to find God but could not, said, "I'm searching for answers I'm never going to get." When confronted with the reality of eventual death, a Jewish man replied, "Who knows what it will be?" Not being able to find answers, these Jewish people and others devote their energies to the material things of this life to try to find something to live for and to satisfy them. We have the answer for the spiritual need of every heart. It is found in the Bible that gives the pathway to lead sinful souls to faith in Messiah Jesus and salvation in him. In our personal relationship with the Lord, we have the answers to the questions of life, death, and eternity. Our blessed task is to reach these dear Jews and Gentiles with the message of redemption. Let us do it, today!

Making It Personal

1. Do most Jews and Gentiles believe in God and the Bible? Why?

2. What two things are necessary for an effective witness? Romans 10:1.

3. What three basic truths can you share to show the Bible is true?

4. What is internal evidence? Give Scriptural references.

5. What is external evidence? Give two illustrations.

6. What is personal experience? Give illustrations from the text and your life.

7. How can you challenge an atheist to seek God?

8. Is the Jewish Bible arranged differently than your Bible? How?

9. Are all translations of the Bible the same? Why is this important?

Additional Bible Verses for Study

- Psalm 19:14
- Zechariah 8:16
- John 8:32, 14:6
- Deuteronomy 8:4
- Matthew 4:4
- Colossians 1:5

Eternity

PART A
Heaven

Most people think about death and what will happen after they die. Since they have no answers to their questions, and they do not know what the afterlife holds for them, they prefer not to dwell upon it. Some say there is nothing after this life, and when they die, that is the end of everything. Regardless of what people think, all will admit that we are headed relentlessly toward death and it will happen someday. As true Christians, we must endeavor to help lost souls understand that there is life after death, and it is a very real life. Every person must prepare now for what is coming in the afterlife. Almighty God has given in the Bible the information we need to make the right decisions to equip us to face death and eternity. When we walk in the path that God has laid out for us, the fear of death is gone, and we face a wonderful future!

There are serious warnings in the Bible about the result of men and women ignoring or rejecting what God has said to us on this most important subject. I am certain that as we prayerfully share God's Word with Jewish people and Gentiles, we will find many who will listen to God's plan for their lives. We know how it feels to be forgiven of our sins when we confess our sins to

God and ask for his forgiveness on the basis of what Jesus did for us on the cross. We have the absolute assurance of going to heaven when we die. The peace of God that comes to the believing heart is beyond human definition. Our friends, Jews and Gentiles, need to know also!

When we stood at the gravesites of our spouses, we knew that Doris and Rich were in heaven beyond any question or doubt. They both believed God's Word and knew Jesus as their Savior. Peace surrounds Bible-believers when they are called to go through the valley of the shadow of death. Families are sustained by the promises of God when death takes a loved one from our midst. We need to learn Bible verses that tell us about heaven so we can show unbelievers the way. May the following Holy Scriptures encourage you in your walk with the Lord and give you wisdom to share the gospel with lost souls. Most of the Holy Scriptures we will study are found in the Jewish Bible. Except for Orthodox and Hasidic Jews, and perhaps a number of Conservatives, my experience has been that Jews do not read their Bible. In many Jewish Bibles, they give a schedule of readings for the holidays, holydays and other times of the year. These *Haftorah* readings are limited and do not include the prophecies about the coming of the Messiah. Jews who practice Reform and Reconstructionist Judaism do not read the Bible, for they have no faith in the Bible as the Word of God. Most of these Jews do not believe in God. From my experience of 59 years in sharing God's Word with the children of Israel, I know that most Jewish people have little or no knowledge of the Jewish Holy Scriptures (Old Testament).

If we do not tell them, Jewish people will never know God's plan of redemption in Messiah Jesus. They will know nothing about heaven and hell.

> Study to show thyself approved unto God, a workman that needeth not to be ashamed, rightly dividing the word of truth.
>
> 2 Timothy 2:15

The Old Testament teaches that there is a wonderful place called heaven. There are many verses in the Bible that speak of heaven.

Psalm 11:4—"The LORD is in his holy temple, the LORD'S throne is in heaven: his eyes behold, his eyelids try, the children of men." God's throne is in his holy temple in heaven.

Psalm 103:19—"The LORD hath prepared his throne in the heavens; and his kingdom ruleth over all." God made his throne in the heavens from which he rules over the world. This is a literal throne in a real heaven.

Psalm 110:1—"The LORD said unto my Lord, Sit thou at my right hand, until I make thine enemies thy footstool." This is a reference to Messiah Jesus who, after his death and resurrection, ascended to the right hand of God the

Father in heaven. This is God's throne in heaven. Messiah Jesus sat down at the right hand of God the Father.

2 Chronicles 18:18—"Again he said, Therefore hear the word of the LORD; I saw the LORD sitting upon his throne, and all the host of heaven standing on his right hand and on his left." There are hosts of people and angels standing about the throne of God, in heaven. These words were given to the Jewish man of God who was a prophet. The prophet spoke these words to the king of Israel.

2 Samuel 22:7—"In my distress I called upon the LORD, and cried to my God: and he did hear my voice out of his temple, and my cry did enter into his ears." There is a literal temple of God in heaven.

Psalm 23:4, 23:6—"Yea, though I walk through the valley of the shadow of death, I will fear no evil: for thou [God] art with me … Surely goodness and mercy shall follow me all the days of my life: and I will dwell in the house of the LORD for ever." King David of Israel knew Almighty God as Lord of his life. David had the assurance that when he died he would not fear, for God would be with him. King David knew that there was a literal heaven, and after he died, he would live there forever.

Hebrews 12:22–24—"But ye are come unto mount Sion, and unto the city of the living God, the heavenly Jerusalem, and to an innumerable company of angels, To the general assembly … which are written in heaven …" This speaks of the city of the living God in heaven wherein are multitudes of angels. There are also multitudes of people there who have been forgiven of their sins and are part of the general assembly, which is written in heaven.

1 Peter 3:21–22—" … the resurrection of Jesus Christ: who is gone into heaven, and is on the right hand of God; angels and authorities and powers being made subject unto him." Our studies have shown (Isaiah 53, Daniel 9:24–27, Isaiah 7:14, Micah 5:2, Isaiah 48:16–17) that Jesus is the Messiah who took on a human body to accomplish salvation for us. The Messiah is a member of the Godhead as revealed in prophecy in the Old Testament. Messiah Jesus in heaven rules over angels and believers who are there.

Isaiah 26:19—"Thy dead men shall live, together with my dead body shall they arise. Awake and sing, ye that dwell in dust … the earth shall cast out the dead." Isaiah, the greatest of the Jewish prophets, emphatically spoke of the bodily resurrection of men and women who put their faith in God's plan of forgiveness of sin. After death, believers in God will live again and sing! "Thy dead men shall live" means those who belong to God and are a part of his family. The way people become a part of God's family is clearly given in the Bible. Sin separates men and women from God in this life and for eternity after death. Sin can be forgiven only through God's plan for us. When people put their trust in this plan of salvation, Jews and Gentiles will be forgiven of their sins by the blood of atonement provided by Messiah Jesus' death and resurrection.

Colossians 1:12–14—"Giving thanks unto the Father

[God], which hath made us meet to be partakers of the inheritance of the saints in light: Who hath delivered us from the power of darkness, and hath translated us into the kingdom of his dear Son: In whom we have redemption through his blood, even the forgiveness of sins." Many times in the Old Testament it mentions saints as people who have been forgiven of their sins and are living for God—Psalm 30:4, Psalm 132:9, Daniel 7:18, and Zechariah 14:5. When sharing God's Word with Jewish people, we do not use the word saint if we do not have the opportunity to explain it. If saints are mentioned, say, "The word saint or saints is mentioned in the Jewish Bible and it means people who have been forgiven of their sins and are living for the God of Israel. It has nothing to do with a religion."

THE HEAVENS

Both the Old and New Testaments show us that there are three areas above the earth that are called the heavens. The first heaven above us would be the atmosphere and the clouds. The second heaven would be the stars. The third and highest heaven is where we find the throne of Almighty God.

Ezekiel 32:4—"…and will cause all the fowls of the heaven…" The birds live in the first heaven.

Matthew 24:29—"…the stars shall fall from heaven…" This is the second heaven.

Matthew 5:34—"But I say unto you, Swear not at all; neither by heaven; for it is God's throne." This gives us the third heaven where God's throne is located.

Deuteronomy 10:14—"Behold, the heaven and the heaven of heavens is the LORD's thy God, the earth also, with all that therein is." This verse tells us there is heaven and then heavens.

Psalm 11:4—"The LORD is in his holy temple, the LORD's throne is in heaven…" A throne in a temple is a literal place. It is a real dwelling and someday we will see it.

2 Corinthians 12:2, 12:4—"I knew a man in Christ above fourteen years ago… such an one caught up to the third heaven… How he was caught up into paradise [another word for the third heaven—God's throne], and heard unspeakable words, which it is not lawful for a man to utter." This was written by Paul, the Jewish man of God. The third heaven is a real place.

Luke 23:43—"And Jesus said unto him, Verily I say unto thee, Today shalt thou be with me in paradise." When the man who was dying on the cross put his faith in Jesus, Jesus said this newly forgiven sinner, after he died, would be with the Lord in paradise, or heaven. Heaven is the abode of Bible-believers of all ages. We will live for eternity in God's presence in peace and joy. We will also serve the Lord there.

1 Peter 1:3–4—"Blessed be the God and Father of our

Lord Jesus Christ, which according to his abundant mercy hath begotten us again unto a lively hope by the resurrection of Jesus Christ from the dead, To an inheritance incorruptible, and undefiled, and that fadeth not away, reserved in heaven for you." What a wonderful inheritance we have in heaven! Our future in heaven for eternity cannot be corrupted, nor can it be defiled, and it will never fade! Our joy in heaven, after millions of years there, will be the same as it was the day we entered eternity!

Exodus 25:1, 25:8–9—"And the LORD spake unto Moses, saying … And let them make me a sanctuary; that I may dwell among them. According to all that I show thee, after the pattern of the tabernacle, and the pattern of all the instruments thereof, even so shall ye make it." This is a truth that was revealed when God spoke to Moses on Sinai. God told Moses to make the tabernacle like the pattern God showed him of the tabernacle that is in heaven!

Hebrews 9:19–21, 9:23–24—"For when Moses had spoken every precept to all the people according to the law, he took the blood of calves and of goats, with water, and scarlet wool, and hyssop, and sprinkled both the book, and all the people, Saying, This is the blood of the testament [covenant] which God hath enjoined unto you. Moreover he sprinkled with blood both the tabernacle, and all the vessels of the ministry … It was therefore necessary that the patterns of things in the heavens should be purified with these; but the heavenly things themselves with better sacrifices than these. For Christ is not entered into the holy places made with hands, which are the figures of the true; but into heaven itself, now to appear in the presence of God for us." There is a tabernacle in heaven that was not made by human hands but by God. God told Moses to make a tabernacle from the pattern of the one in heaven. Moses' tabernacle was used on earth to provide the place for the Israelites to worship God and find forgiveness for their sins through the blood of atonement. Leviticus 16 gives the detailed instructions for the blood of atonement that was offered on Yom Kippur, the Day of Atonement. This was done once a year for the nation of Israel. In Leviticus 5:5–10 there are instructions for individual Jews to be forgiven of their sins during the year by the blood of atonement.

There is a real tabernacle in heaven. Moses and the Israelites made a pattern of it in the tabernacle on earth. Animal sacrifices provided the blood of atonement for the tabernacle on earth in the years of Moses and following. After his crucifixion and resurrection, the blood of Messiah Jesus that was shed for us to be forgiven of our sins (Isaiah 53) was placed in the tabernacle in heaven! Heaven is a real place.

Revelation 11:19, 15:5—"And the temple of God was opened in heaven, and there was seen in his temple the ark of his testament [covenant]…And after that I looked, and, behold, the temple of the tabernacle of the testimony in heaven was opened." The temple of God is in heaven and the tabernacle is also there. Someday we will see it!

What joy it is to know Messiah Jesus as our Redeemer. The fear of death is gone! Death for us is the doorway to eternal life in heaven forever and ever. We will see the Lord and serve him for all eternity. Let us share the gospel so many lost souls can be saved and be with us in heaven for eternity.

PART B
Hell

This is a subject that is seldom discussed seriously. Both Jewish people and Gentiles, who are not Bible-believers, do not consider the possibility that there is a real place after death that is called hell. Many jokes are shared regarding hell, so the reality of such a place is determined not to exist. The word hell does not enter into conversation of unbelievers, except for being used in humor or cursing. Most people, if they believed in hell, would not know how they could avoid going there after death. Therefore, the most comfortable attitude for unbelievers to have is to ignore the subject. Death is an ever-present reality in families when loved ones or friends die. People wonder, *Where are they? What has happened to them?* As with Gentiles, there are many questions in the minds of Jewish people about death. They do not know where to find answers.

Most Jewish people do not have knowledge of God's

plan of how to be forgiven of their sins. The gospel is foreign to them. Jews have been greatly persecuted through hundreds of years by so-called Christians. It is very difficult for them to discern between what is God's truth, what is just the teaching of a religion concerning sin, how to be forgiven, and the reality of heaven and hell. Many Jewish people and Gentiles just forget about the subject, or do not talk about it, and go on with their daily living. There are Jews who, knowing God's plan of salvation in Messiah Jesus, do not want to accept it. They are taught that if they believe in Jesus, they will no longer be Jews; however, there are many people who, when shown the way of salvation in Messiah Jesus by a loving Bible-believer, will put their trust in the Lord. We must give them the opportunity to be saved.

There are individuals who want to be the so-called masters of their own fate and future. Men and women plan and work toward the goals of being successful and living a long life; however, they can never be certain that they will live to see it. Diets, exercise, doctoring, and medication can help people to live longer, but human beings are not in control of the time that they will die.

It is of the utmost importance that we share with unbelievers what the Bible says about death and what comes after death. Bible references can mean so very much to unsaved Jews as they consider what the God of Israel has said to them. Bible verses will help you as you share the gospel with Jews, your unsaved family members, neighbors, or those with whom you work.

The way of life is above to the wise, that he may depart from hell [*Sheol*] beneath.

Proverbs 15:24

There are three words in the original text of the Bible that tell us where people will go after they die. These words are translated hell in most verses of the Bible. The Old Testament word for hell in Hebrew is *Sheol.* In the New Testament, hell is translated from the Greek words *Hades* and *Gehenna. Sheol* of the Old Testament became *Hades* in the New Testament. They are the same place; however, there is a change in the inhabitants of *Hades* after the death and resurrection of Jesus. *Sheol* and *Hades* have two dwelling places that were separated from each other by a great gulf. Souls could not pass from one place to the other. The people who died with their sins forgiven by God went to the righteous side of *Sheol* or *Hades* where they lived in peace and God's provision. In Luke 23:39–43 Jesus told the repentant sinner on the cross that he would be with him in Paradise after he died. Ephesians 4:7–10 tells us that after his death on the cross, Christ (Messiah) Jesus went down to the lower parts of the earth, where *Hades* is located. He then took the righteous from all ages out of *Hades* and up to the highest heaven and gave gifts to his faithful people. The sinners, on the side of *Sheol,* or *Hades* for the unbelievers, would continue in their suffering there until the Great White Throne Judgment after which they would be cast into hell (*Gehenna*).

Gehenna is actually eternal hell. It is mentioned by Jesus eleven times, such as in Matthew 10:28, "And fear not them which kill the body, but are not able to kill the soul: but rather fear him which is able to destroy both soul and body in hell [*Gehenna*]." The Bible says that the fear of man can keep lost people from considering the gospel. These unbelievers cannot destroy a person's soul. Life can be terminated by death on earth, but the body and soul will exist in hell (*Gehenna*) forever with great suffering. The unbeliever's life that was lived on earth will not be available in hell. It will be destroyed. The sinner will not have the same quality of life as here on earth. The sinner in hell (*Gehenna*) for eternity will still have an eternal body and soul that will suffer untold agony.

Jesus gave solemn warning about hell (*Gehenna*). One example is found in Mark 9:43, "… to go into hell [*Gehenna*] into the fire that never shall be quenched." May God speak to our hearts to stir us, challenge us, and change our priorities as we see what hell really will be for those who die with sin in their lives.

Does God, through the Jewish prophets, tell the children of Israel that there will be eternal punishment for those who have rejected God's plan of salvation and die in their sins? Yes! We read in Isaiah 33:14, "The sinners in Zion are afraid; fearfulness hath surprised the hypocrites. Who among us shall dwell with the devouring fire? Who among us shall dwell with everlasting burnings?" These are solemn words of warning. Isaiah's people were the Jewish people. To dwell is to live. The sinners in Zion (Jews and Gentiles) will be afraid and fearful. Their sins will cast them into fire and everlasting burnings. There will be no atheist in hell. When a person is in hell, it will be too late to repent and be forgiven of sin. Decisions that affect eternity must be made while we are still alive here on earth.

There are different translations of the Hebrew word *Sheol* in Jewish Bibles and other versions. In the King James Version, *Sheol* is translated as hell in Old Testament verses. In Jewish Bibles, *Sheol* is translated the grave, the nether world, or sometimes hell. For Jewish people today, *Sheol* usually would not mean hell, or a place of suffering. Hell is not a part of Jewish teaching. The suffering of sinners after death in hell is in Jewish Bibles in Isaiah 33:14 and other verses, but it is not taught in Jewish places of worship. Remember, Isaiah was the greatest of the Jewish prophets. God gave Israel the truth through Isaiah.

What does the Bible teach concerning *Sheol?* After death, do people have consciousness? In the Bible, God gave us the example of judgment upon Egypt and King Pharoah. In Ezekiel 31:2 and 31:16–17 we read,

> Son of man, speak unto Pharoah king of Egypt, and to his multitude…I made the nations to shake at the sound of his fall, when I cast him down to hell [*Sheol*] with them that descend into the pit…They also went down into hell [*Sheol*] with him unto them that be slain with the sword…

Continuing in Ezekiel 32:21 and 32:31,

> The strong among the mighty shall speak to him out of the midst of hell [*Sheol*] with them that help him: they are gone down, they lie

uncircumcised, slain by the sword.... Pharoah shall see them, and shall be comforted over all his multitude, even Pharaoh and all his army slain by the sword, saith the LORD God.

What do we learn from these verses of Scripture? Pharoah and his army are slain in battle and go down to *Sheol*. In Ezekiel 31 and 32, the armies of other nations also die in battle and descend to the pit, which is the same place as *Sheol*. What do we learn about *Sheol*? After King Pharoah and his army died and were buried, they are in *Sheol*. People speak out of the midst of *Sheol*. "Pharoah shall see them" means that he had eyesight in *Sheol*. Pharoah was comforted over the death of his army when he saw the death of the armies that slew his soldiers. Pharoah had emotions and memory in *Sheol*. After Pharoah died and was buried, he had the same emotions and eyesight that he had when he was alive on earth. The emotions would have come from his memory of the battles on earth where his army was slaughtered. There is life after death!

The Jewish man of God, Isaiah, recorded the Word of God in Isaiah 14:9–17,

Hell [*Sheol*] from beneath is moved for thee to meet thee at thy coming: it stirreth up the dead for thee, even all the chief ones of the earth ... All they shall speak and say unto thee, Art thou also become weak as we? Art thou become like unto us? Thy pomp is brought down to the grave ...

The word grave is in the text, but the Hebrew is *Sheol*. In these verses in Isaiah, we learn that there is life in *Sheol*. People speak to one another and are weak in *Sheol*.

In 2 Samuel 22:6 we read, "The sorrows of hell [*Sheol*] compassed me about." Psalm 116:3 tells us, "… and the pains of hell [*Sheol*] got hold upon me: I found trouble and sorrow." These verses in the Bible clearly state that in *Sheol* there is sorrow, pain and trouble.

The Jewish King Solomon recorded in Proverbs 5:4–5 and 7:27 further truth regarding *Sheol*, "But her end is bitter as wormwood, sharp as a two-edged sword. Her feet go down to death; her steps take hold on hell [*Sheol*] … Her house is the way to hell [*Sheol*], going down to the chambers of death." God tells us in these verses of his Word that this person's sinful life would lead her to death and then to suffering in *Sheol*.

There is another truth that we must understand in order for us to have a clear picture of *Sheol*. *Sheol* is not just a place of suffering for the ungodly who die in their sins. *Sheol* was made of two parts that were separated by a great gulf that no person could pass over. One part of *Sheol* was the abode of those who died with sin in their lives; they entered a place of suffering. The other part was the abode of the righteous whose sin was forgiven by God while they were alive on earth. These people had repented, asked God for his forgiveness, and had the blood of atonement to be cleansed of all sin. These believers lived in peace and joy.

King David of Israel recorded the following in Psalm 16:8–11,

I have set the LORD always before me: because he is at my right hand, I shall not be moved. Therefore my heart is glad, and my glory rejoiceth: my flesh also shall rest in hope. For thou [God] wilt not leave my soul in hell [*Sheol*]; neither wilt thou suffer thine Holy One to see corruption. [King David foretells the resurrection of God's Holy One who is the Messiah. King David's body did see corruption in the grave but the one David speaks of would not see corruption.] Thou wilt show me the path of life: in thy presence is fullness of joy; at thy right hand there are pleasures for evermore.

King David had the assurance that in this life and after he died, he would have fullness of joy and pleasures forever in the presence of God. He knew that though his soul would be in *Sheol* for a time, after that he would dwell with God for eternity in heaven. In David's life on earth and after physical death, he would have great joy and pleasure forever.

According to my earnest expectation and my hope, that in nothing I shall be ashamed, but that with all boldness, as always, so now also Christ shall be magnified in my body, whether it be by life, or by death. For to me to live is Christ, and to die is gain.

Philippians 1:20–21

A clear picture of *Hades* is given to us in Luke 16:19–31. This portion of God's Word records for us the words of Jesus. The Scripture does not say that this was a parable. It is a true account given by Jesus about real people. It is a stern warning for all people to seek God's forgiveness of their sins while they still have time. We read,

> There was a certain rich man, [This just happened to be a rich man, but the following could happen to any man or woman.] which was clothed in purple and fine linen, and fared sumptuously every day: [He had the life that so many covet today—financial security with all the comforts he desired.] And there was a certain beggar named Lazarus, which was laid at his gate, full of sores, And desiring to be fed with the crumbs which fell from the rich man's table: moreover the dogs came and licked his sores. [Lazarus was a poor, sick man with nothing of this world's goods. There is quite a contrast between these two men as far as worldly possessions and position is concerned.] And it came to pass, that the beggar died, and was carried by the angels into Abraham's bosom: the rich man also died, and was buried. And in hell [*Hades* which is the same as *Sheol* in the Old Testament] he lift up his eyes, being in torments, and seeth Abraham afar off, and Lazarus in his bosom ...

This is a startling picture of contrasts. The position these two men had upon earth is now dramatically reversed.

They both died. We will see that the riches of the affluent man meant nothing after death. The poor situation of the man who had nothing of this world's goods now is turned around, and he has everything he needs for an eternity filled with peace and God's provision!

Lazarus, the poor, sick man, is now in perfect health in the presence of Abraham. Notice that when Lazarus died, he was carried by angels to be with Abraham in a wonderful new dwelling place. Psalm 23:4 encourages believers with the truth that God will be with us and comfort us when we die and pass from this life to heaven. Luke 16:25 says that Lazarus was comforted in his new life. What joy, peace, and rejoicing must have been in the life of Lazarus in his new home! The old, very hard life that he had on earth is now a thing of the past—it is gone. He is in the presence of the family of God. His abode is still called *Hades,* but he is in the part where the righteous live.

As we mentioned before, we know that this place to which people went after physical death had two different parts. One part was for those whose sins had been forgiven. Though the text does not say that Lazarus' sins had been cleansed, we know this is true by the fact that Lazarus went to where Abraham was. Abraham was called the friend of God and certainly was in the place of the righteous.

The man who had all of the earthly possessions and riches he could desire, also died and was buried. Again we read in Luke 16:23 and following,

> And in hell [*Hades*] he lift up his eyes, being in torments, and seeth Abraham afar off, and Lazarus in his bosom. And he cried and said, Father Abraham, have mercy on me, and send Lazarus, that he may dip the tip of his finger in water, and cool my tongue; for I am tormented in this flame.

We are now given greater understanding as to just what it is like in *Hades* for people who die in their sins. This would be the same as in the Old Testament Scriptures that gave us a picture of suffering, sorrow and pain in *Sheol.* Jews and Gentiles will suffer the same fate if they die in their sins.

This man who called upon Abraham had all of his senses that he had when he was alive on earth. He could feel for he was tormented in this flame. He recognized Lazarus and spoke of him by name, so he had memory. He also knew Abraham was a great distance away. How he knew Abraham is not mentioned, but he had knowledge of Abraham. He "lifted up his eyes … and seeth Abraham … and Lazarus" so he had eyes to see. He desired water to cool his tongue and relieve his pain, so he had a tongue and knew what cool water could do for him. He cried for relief, so he had emotions. Lazarus also had a full body for the man in suffering spoke of the finger of Lazarus.

The fact that people cannot go from the wicked, suffering side of *Hades* to the place where the righteous live is given in Luke 16:25–26,

> But Abraham said, Son, remember that thou in thy lifetime receivedst thy good things, and likewise Lazarus evil things: but now he is comforted, and thou are tormented. And beside all this, between us and you there is a great gulf fixed: so that they which would pass from hence to you cannot; neither can they pass to us, that would come from thence.

Decisions regarding sin, the forgiveness of sin and eternity are made in this life. There is no second chance after death. There are people who believe that there is a chance that they will go to heaven after they have spent some time of suffering some place after death. There are religions that say there is a second chance. Some teach that everyone will go to heaven eventually. There is no place in God's Word that gives any basis for this false hope. Sinners who never trusted in God's plan of salvation will not have a second chance to be forgiven of their sins after they die. Hebrews 9:27, "And as it is appointed unto men once to die, but after this the judgment." We must warn people, in love, to seek the truth about life after death before it is too late!

Have you ever heard a person say, "If I saw someone come back from the dead, then I would believe"? God speaks to this issue in Luke 16:27–31,

> Then he [the man in the suffering side of *Hades*] said, I pray thee therefore, father [Abraham], that thou wouldest send him [Lazarus] to my father's house: For I have five brethren; that he may testify unto them, lest they also come into this place of

torment. Abraham saith unto him, They have Moses and the prophets; let them hear them. And he said, Nay, father Abraham: but if one went unto them from the dead, they will repent. And he [Abraham] said unto him, If they hear not Moses and the prophets, neither will they be persuaded, though one rose from the dead.

This man in torment remembered his five brothers on earth who were unbelievers. He said his brothers would not believe Moses, the prophets, or God's Word in the Bible; however, if one rose from the dead and testified to them, they would believe. Abraham said his brothers would not believe the words of one who rose from the dead! Notice that the sinner in suffering spoke of his brothers and their need to repent. This is the message we must give to sinful souls.

What an awesome responsibility this places upon us. As the Lord continues to give us life and breath, we must share the gospel with lost souls at every opportunity that is given to us. We must not go about life as usual and do nothing to help lost people know the gospel by which they can be saved!

> I charge thee therefore before God, and the Lor d Jesus Christ, who shall judge the quick and the dead at his appearing and his kingdom; Preach the word; be instant in season, out of season; reprove, rebuke, exhort with all longsuffering and doctrine.
>
> 2 Timothy 4:1–2

There are many Scriptures you can share with lost souls concerning death and eternity. Revelation 20:11–15 is very important. It deals with *Gehenna,* or eternal hell.

> And I saw a great white throne, and him that sat on it, from whose face the earth and the heaven [the lowest heaven] fled away; and there was found no place for them. And I saw the dead, small and great, stand before God; and the books were opened: and another book was opened, which is the book of life: and the dead were judged out of those things which were written in the books, according to their works. And the sea gave up the dead which were in it; and death and hell [this would be *Hades*] delivered up the dead which were in them: and they were judged every man according to their works. And death and hell [*Hades*] were cast into the lake of fire. This is the second death. And whosoever was not found written in the book of life was cast into the lake of fire.

This is God's final judgment of people who died with unforgiven sin in their lives. Sinners in *Hades* are brought to this Great White Throne Judgment where they are cast into everlasting fire and punishment. Revelation 21:8, "But the fearful, and unbelieving, and the abominable, and murderers, and whoremongers, and sorcerers, and idolaters, and all liars, shall have their part in the lake which burneth with fire and brimstone: which is the second death." Most people do not commit the horrible crimes that are mentioned in this verse; however, notice that included in those who will spend eternity in hell are the unbelieving, those who did not believe the gospel, and all liars. Romans 3:23 tells us, "For all have sinned, and come short of the glory of God." In Romans 5:8–9 we read, "But God commendeth his love toward us, in that, while we were yet sinners, Christ [Messiah] died for us. Much more then, being now justified by his [Jesus] blood, we shall be saved from wrath through him."

Lost souls must find their peace with God through his plan of salvation. There is no other way. We must tell them how to be saved. Many will not believe, but there are many Jews and Gentiles who will put their trust in Messiah Jesus, if we share God's Word with them in a way that they can understand. The Lord wants you to witness. Jesus will help you. The Holy Spirit will give you the words. Let's do it!

Making It Personal—Part A

1. Explain what the Jewish Bible teaches us about a real, literal heaven. Is there more than one heaven?

2. Who is in heaven?

3. What did God show to Moses on Mount Sinai?

4. What was the purpose of the Jewish tabernacle? Is there a tabernacle that means something to us? Explain your answer.

5. What Jewish people, whom we know from the Jewish

Bible, had the assurance that they would see God in heaven after their death?

6. How can Jews and Gentiles be certain of going to heaven when they die?

Additional Bible Verses for Study—Part A

- 2 Corinthians 5:1, 5:6, 5:8–9
- Revelation 4:1–11
- Revelation 5:1, 5:5–14
- Revelation 7:9–15
- Revelation 22:1–5

Making It Personal—Part B

1. What will happen to people who die who have not trusted in God's plan of salvation?

2. What is *Sheol, Hades,* and *Gehenna?*

3. What do Jewish people believe about hell? What does the Jewish prophet Isaiah tell us in Isaiah 33:14?

4. What do we learn about *Sheol* and Pharoah and his army that is recorded by the Jewish prophet Ezekiel in 31:2, 31:16–17, 32:21, and 32:31?

5. What does King David of Israel tell us about Sheol in Psalm 16:8–11?

6. In the New Testament, Jesus spoke of *Hades* and two men in Luke 16:19–31. What key truths do we learn from this passage of God's Word?

7. What do we learn about *Gehenna* in Revelation 20:11–15 and 21:8?

8. Will what you learned about hell give you a greater burden to share the gospel with lost souls? Will you witness for Jesus?

9. Practice witnessing with someone in your small group talking about heaven and hell.

George and Jean Gruen

Additional Bible Verses for Study—Part B

The most important verses you need to know about life after death for unsaved people have been given in this study. Memorize the references given from the Old Testament and the New Testament about *Sheol*, *Hades*, and *Gehenna*. Use these verses as the Spirit of God leads you to share your faith in Messiah (Christ) Jesus.

Special Tracts and CDs
for Your Witness

When sharing your faith with Jewish people, it is good to use special tracts, CDs, cassette tapes and books that have been prepared with the needs of Jews in mind. Many times you will meet a seeking heart, but you will not have time to share the complete gospel message. In such situations, always leave a tract that will give God's plan of salvation from Old Testament prophecy and the New Testament fulfillments in Jesus. When it has been our privilege to talk with our Jewish people for just a few minutes, we always knew that the tract we left with them would give the Bible verses needed for them to put their trust in Jesus.

If a general gospel tract from your church is used, it might include words and phrases that make it difficult for a person of Jewish upbringing to read with a receptive heart and mind. In our study on terminology to use in witnessing, we considered a number of words that could hinder a Jew from being open to a gospel witness. Saying Christian, Christ, church, cross, Trinity, converting, etc., will bring to the Jewish mind thoughts of anti-Semitism, persecution, the Holocaust, and many other atrocities the Jews have suffered. When this happens, they most likely will turn away from your endeavor to share the Word of God with them. You can understand why it is important to have gospel materials that have been prepared for Jewish people.

> The Lor d gave the word: great was the company of those that published it.
>
> Psalm 68:11

In our years of sharing God's way of salvation with our Jewish people, George has written a number of special tracts and recorded messages on CDs for distribution to Jewish people. You can also obtain tracts from any good tract supply or Bible bookstore. As we mentioned previously, if you are sharing these tracts with Jewish people, please read the tract through thoroughly so that the words that are offensive to Jewish people are not found in the tract. You can see contact information at the end of this book for details on how you can obtain our tracts and CDs that you desire to use in witnessing.

(1) SHALOM—PEACE IN THESE TIMES

This is the first tract that George wrote many years ago. It has been distributed throughout the United States and overseas. It appeals to Jewish people because of *"Shalom"* in Hebrew and the Star of David on the cover. The title of "Peace in These Times" is relevant for our day because of the many problems that people face. They are trying to find peace in the midst of distressing circumstances. They will read or listen to anything that might help them to find answers to their difficult situations. Many Jews and Gentiles have a longing in their hearts for real, lasting peace, but they do not know where to find it. Material possessions can provide some pleasure and enjoyment, but things are not the answer and will not bring peace to the heart, spirit, and soul. True, lasting peace comes only from Almighty God.

The message of this tract deals with the fact that every person has sinned. Ecclesiastes 7:20 in the Old Testament gives this basic truth, "For there is not a just [good] man upon earth, that doeth good, and sinneth not." We read in Romans 3:23, "For all have sinned, and come short of the glory of God." Sin separates people from God and his peace. Isaiah 59:1–2 reads, "Behold, the LORD'S hand is not shortened, that it cannot save; neither his ear heavy, that it cannot hear: But your iniquities have separated between you and your God, and your sins have hid his face from you, that he will not hear." Sin separates men and women from God. The ultimate end of sin leads lost souls to eternal separation from God in hell. A verse that bears repeating is Revelation 21:8, which says, "But the fearful, and unbelieving, and the abominable, and murderers, and whoremongers, and sorcerers, and idolaters, and all liars, shall have their part in the lake which burneth with fire and brimstone: which is the second death." The first death is physical, with separation from this life on earth. The second death is separation from God with suffering in hell for all eternity.

> But the word of the Lord endureth for ever. And this is the word which by the gospel is preached unto you.
>
> 1 Peter 1:25

God's plan of redemption for lost souls is made clear from its beginning in Genesis to the cleansing of sin through the blood of atonement. The Godhead is presented from Scriptures to show that Messiah Jesus is one in the Godhead. Prophecies from the Jewish men of God in the Bible lead souls to see that Jesus is their promised Messiah and the one who would provide the once for all time blood of atonement. Isaiah 53 is printed in its entirety to show that the coming of Messiah Jesus to the world was foretold by this Jewish man of God seven hundred years before Jesus lived here on earth.

The two comings of Messiah to earth are also given with Scriptures to confirm this great truth: his first coming to bring personal peace to individuals and his second coming to bring peace to Israel and the world. New Testament verses are given to show Jesus is our promised Messiah. Jews are urged to accept Jesus as Messiah and Savior. George is Jewish because his father was Jewish. The Jewish Bible teaches that lineage is determined by the father. This is seen in the life of Joseph in Egypt and also in the life of Moses. George can say to anyone with perfect clarity that he was born a Jew and will die as a Jewish Bible-believer. You, too, can say that you were born German, Russian, Italian, etc. and will die as a German,

Russian, or Italian Bible-believer. Your heritage should have no bearing on your faith.

(2) HAVE YOU DISCOVERED THE PRINCIPLES FOR PERSONAL PEACE?

A Star of David highlights the cover. It does attract attention. This is a ten-page booklet that is designed to be read with an unbeliever or to be used for general distribution. The tract is printed in two sizes. The larger size is in very large print to be given to an older person who might have difficulty reading. The large print is also good for sharing the gospel with Jewish people in their home or yours. You can place it on a table and turn the pages as each principle is presented. Ample time should be given to go over each principle to discuss it and ask for questions. The left side of the open tract gives the principle and Bible verses to prove it. The Scripture verses are from the Old Testament. On the right side of the tract, there is a drawing to illustrate the truth presented.

Principle 1   The plan of the God of Abraham, Isaac, and Jacob.
God loves you.
God has a plan for personal peace for you.

Principle 2   My sin has separated me from God's peace.
All have sinned.
Sin separates us from God now and for eternity.

Principle 3   God has provided the way to be forgiven
               of sin.
               Old Testament times—animal sacrifice.
               Today—Messiah.
               Foretold in the Old Testament.
               Fulfilled in Messiah Jesus.

Principle 4   Faith and repentance make forgiveness a
               reality.
               Take these steps:
                   1. Believe God's plan.
                   2. Confess your sin to God.
                   3. Receive Messiah into your life.
                   4. A sample prayer is given.

Steps to Draw Closer to God:
               •   Pray daily.
               •   Read your Bible.
               •   Share your faith.
               •   Be with believers.

A Jewish man wrote to us from the Pittsburgh,
Pennsylvania, area. He said he grew up in a Jewish
home, had his Bar Mitzvah, and as an adult Jew he was a
mechanical engineer. With his letter, he enclosed a copy
of the small-size "Have You Discovered the Principles
for Personal Peace?" He wrote that a man had given him
this booklet. He read it and at 2:00 a.m. on Saturday (he
also gave us the date and his home address) he prayed the
prayer at the end of the tract to accept Jesus as his Messiah
and Redeemer. He gave the name of the Christian man

who sent him the tract. His desire now was to give the Word of God to others so he asked for a supply of this tract. Praise the Lord! Let the Lord use you to distribute gospel tracts to seeking Jewish hearts.

We gave our seminar on how Christians can witness to Jewish people at a church near Washington, D.C. After the presentation, an eighteen-year-old Christian young man came up to our display and took the large-print copy of "Have You Discovered the Principles for Personal Peace." He said that this large-print tract was just what he needed. He was witnessing to an elderly Jewish woman who could not see very well. We have given this large-print tract to Jewish men and women ages eighty-eight, ninety, ninety-one, ninety-four, and ninety-five. They gladly accepted the tracts!

> Thy word is a lamp unto my feet, and a light unto my path.
>
> Psalm 119:105

(3) WHO IS A JEW?

Jewish people for many years have had debates about the question, "Who is a Jew?" They have been taught that if a person's mother is Jewish, then the son or daughter is Jewish. According to the Jewish Bible, a person was a Hebrew, or Jewish, if the father was a Hebrew. The best illustration of this is Joseph (Abraham, Isaac, Jacob, and then Joseph). No Jewish person would ever say that Joseph was not a Jew. When Joseph was sold into slavery in Egypt, Almighty God brought events to pass that brought Joseph to the second highest position in Egypt. He was second only to Pharoah (Genesis 41:39–43). Whom did Joseph marry? In Genesis 41:45 Pharoah gave Asenath, the daughter of an Egyptian priest, to be Joseph's wife. Asenath was an Egyptian Gentile. She was not a Hebrew nor was she Jewish. In Genesis 41:50–52, we learn that as a result of their marriage, they had two sons, Manasseh and Ephraim. Were these two sons Gentiles or Jews? Joseph's sons were definitely Jewish. We know this because when the Jewish people came out of Egypt and went into the Promised Land, the twelve tribes were led by Hebrew leaders. Two of the twelve tribes were led by Manasseh and Ephraim! There is no way that the Hebrew people would have had two Gentiles lead two of their tribes into the Promised Land.

Another illustration of children being Jewish because of the father, and not the mother, was Moses. In Exodus 2:15–22 and 4:20–26, we see that Moses married a Gentile woman and they had a son Gershom. Verse 20 tells us that they had sons. It is evident from the text that Gershom was not circumcised, and because of this, God was angry with Moses. When they went to circumcise Gershom, Moses' wife, Zipporah, was angry at having to do this Jewish rite, something that Gentiles did not do. Their other son must have also been circumcised, perhaps by Moses. Moses' sons were Jewish, even though their mother was Gentile. This is also true of Boaz who married Ruth who was a Gentile from the land of Moab (Ruth 4:10–17). Their son Obed was the father of Jesse who was the father of David. All sons were Jews, not Gentiles! Share this truth with your Jewish contact if the question is raised.

Our tract, "Who Is a Jew?" was written to show Jewish people that they still are Jews when they put their trust in Messiah Jesus. The scriptural content of this tract is basically the same as "Peace in These Times." It gives the way of forgiveness of sins through faith in Messiah Jesus who provided the blood of atonement for us. The Bible verses give the foundation needed for a Jewish person to believe and still be Jewish.

Our radio ministry reaches southern New Jersey over WVCH, 74 on the AM dial, 10:00 a.m. on Saturday. An eighty-one-year-old Jewish woman was listening to this Christian radio station during the week but never on Saturday. She came to the place where she knew that Jesus was the Jewish Messiah; however, she would not accept him. She felt that if she did, she would no longer be a Jew. One Saturday, she turned her radio to WVCH for the first time. She tuned in just when our *Truth for Israel* broadcast was on. Our message told her that when a Jewish person believes in Jesus, that man or woman is still a Jew! After a short period of time reading our tracts and corresponding with us, she accepted Jesus as her Messiah and Savior. Her letters that followed ended with "in the love of Jesus." She attended a fundamental church and was a blessing to many people. This dear Jewish woman went to be with her Savior in heaven at age eighty-six. As the Lord leads, be certain to give a Jewish person a Bible tract and then pray for the salvation of that precious soul.

> Being born again, not of corruptible seed, but of incorruptible, by the Word of God, which liveth and abideth forever.
>
> 1 Peter 1:23

(4) *YESHUA* IN THE *TENACH*

Another objection that Jewish people have to accepting Jesus is that they say the name Jesus is not mentioned in their Bible or the Old Testament. *Not true!* The name Jesus is in the Old Testament in the Hebrew text. Jesus is the English translation of the Hebrew word *Yeshua*. Both words mean salvation or Savior. This tract makes this truth very clear from verses in the Old Testament. Distribute this tract to help Jewish people understand that Jesus is *Yeshua* in their Bibles.

(5) CDS

George personally recorded all of our CDs. You can use these for your study or give them to Jewish people. The recordings were made with unsaved Jews in mind, so do not hesitate to distribute them. You will also learn from the audio how to pronounce Jewish words that you have become familiar with in our studies. All CDs are divided into separate IDs or sections so that you can listen to any section you want without having to go back to the beginning.

Volume 1

• The Life of the Messiah Foretold

This is a detailed study of Isaiah 53:1–12. Jewish people need to understand what this great prophecy foretells about Jesus. It was written about seven hundred years before Messiah Jesus came to earth. His birth, life, death, and resurrection for us to be forgiven of our sins are clearly seen in this Old Testament Scripture. The prophecy reveals to us that Jesus is the promised Messiah and Redeemer who was sent from God the Father for our salvation.

Volume 2

• The Atonement Today

This study gives a clear picture of where we find the blood of atonement today. Through the blood of Messiah Jesus, God forgives us of our sins. Inquirers will learn how the Old Testament atonement, that was given by God through Moses, is now found in Jesus' death and resurrection.

Let's Witness to Jews

• Two Comings of the Messiah

As we have studied, the Messiah comes to earth two times. Messiah comes the first time to bring personal peace for us through the atonement. The second time he will come to bring peace to the world. An effective witness to Jewish people must include this vital truth. The main reason Jewish people do not accept Jesus as their Messiah is that Jesus did not bring peace to Israel and the world when he came. They do not know of the two comings of the Messiah; we must tell them! Give this CD to seeking Jewish hearts.

• How King David Found Peace with God

Jewish people do not want to convert and believe in Jesus. This study makes it clear that King David of Israel believed in being converted. For King David, to convert was to turn from living in sin to living for God after obtaining God's forgiveness of his sins.

Volume 3

• Have You Discovered the Principles for Personal Peace?

This CD gives the principles of how people can be forgiven of sin according to God's directions given in the Bible. The way to find true peace with God is given step-by-step. A sinner can be brought to salvation through listening to this recording.

- ### When Will Messiah Come?

The time in history, or the year, when the Messiah would come to earth to die for our sins is given in a verse-by-verse study of the prophecy of Daniel 9:24–27. Other events in history are also foretold.

- ### The God of Israel

Jewish people find it hard to accept Jesus as deity for they do not believe he is one in the Trinity or Godhead. This study clearly shows in the Old Testament that the God of Israel is revealed to us as God the Father, God the Messiah, and God the Holy Spirit.

Volume 4

- ### How to Have a Personal Relationship with God

Our relationship with Almighty God is not determined by our good works or deeds. Jews and Gentiles must have the blood of atonement that God provided for people to be forgiven of their sins. Ezekiel 33 is studied and tells us that good works or deeds will not take away our sins. We all need Jesus as our Savior.

- ### Who Is a Jew?

The question "Who is a Jew?" has been debated in Jewish circles for many years. This CD answers this question from the Bible. Jews are taught that if the mother is Jewish, then the children are also Jews. The Bible gives us God's Word on this matter.

• Who Is Responsible for the Death of Jesus?

Jewish people have been persecuted for hundreds of years and have been called "Christ killers." Because of this, many Jews will not accept Jesus as their Savior. This accusation has been rescinded by churches; however, it still might be in the minds of Jews who have suffered from this in the past. This audio will give you the answer to this problem if it arises.

> That ye may be mindful of the words which were spoken before by the holy prophets, and of the commandment of us the apostles of the Lord and Saviour.
>
> 2 Peter 3:2

DISTRIBUTING TRACTS AND CDS

When the Lord gives you an opportunity to share your faith in Messiah Jesus, it is always good to have tracts and CDs with you to leave with the inquirer. It is easy to give a tract or CD. Just say, "I know a Jewish man who has a relationship with the God of Israel that has given him great peace. He is older and has been through much. One terrible family experience was his uncle Herman being killed in the Holocaust at the Buchenwald Camp in Germany in World War II. This Jewish Bible-believer shares his experience with God in pamphlets that he has written as well as recorded on CDs. I obtained some of these and would like you to go over this pamphlet (or CD). Let me know what you think about it when I see you again." If there is a table nearby, place the tract or CD on the table and leave. Do not hand the Bible material to the Jewish person unless you have to. If you do, he or she could refuse to accept it, saying they have seen it before or they are just not interested. Should you write to a Jewish friend or family member, send a tract or CD using the same approach.

Making It Personal

1. What are some differences in the tracts you distribute to Gentiles and to Jews?

2. Are Jewish people, according to Judaism, Jewish if their fathers or mothers are Jewish.

3. What tracts are available to you to give to Jewish inquirers? Is there a good way to distribute tracts and CDs?

4. Is there a tract for Jewish people designed for you to read and discuss with them? Explain.

5. Is there a tract with large print that is good for people who cannot see very well to read?

6. Share how you will use tracts and CDs to reach Jewish people with the gospel.

Additional Bible Verses for Study

- Matthew 28:18–20
- Acts 8:26–38
- 1 Corinthians 2:1–5
- Philippians 2:13–16
- 2 Timothy 2:14–16
- James 1:22–25

Making Openings to Share the Gospel

Over the last nine studies, you have gained much knowledge on how to share your faith in Jesus with Jewish people and Gentiles. Now we need to learn how to make contacts that will give us the opportunities to put to use what we have learned. The Lord by his Spirit desires to witness through us! He will do it if we say, "Here am I, Lord, use me." Much joy awaits Christians as they launch out as God's servants to give his precious gospel to lost souls.

There are various approaches that can be used to begin conversations to share God's Word with needy hearts. Almighty God is not limited to what we share with you in making contacts. As the Lord places unsaved souls in your path, he will give you the words to use as you pray and look to him for direction. The Spirit of God might bring to your remembrance what you have studied in these sessions, or he might do a new thing to meet the need of a Jewish person or Gentile. We do not know what is in the hearts and minds of those to whom we witness, but the Lord knows. Be much in prayer for the guidance of the Holy Spirit. This is God's work to be done in his way for his glory. When you begin a new week, ask the Lord to bring to you just the person or persons that he wants you to speak to, and then be ready to be Jesus' ambassador to needy hearts.

> Let the words of my mouth, and the meditation
> of my heart, be acceptable in thy sight, O LORD,
> my strength, and my redeemer.
>
> Psalm 19:14

1. RELATIVES

You have no doubt been surprised when someone in your family marries an unsaved Jewish person. About fifty-seven percent of Jewish people marry outside of the Jewish faith. Throughout history, our Jewish people have endeavored to have their sons and daughters marry Jews. Why then is there such a great number who marry outside of Judaism? We believe this is because the teaching in the synagogues and Jewish temples has not met the spiritual need of the Jewish people. Except for the Orthodox, Hassidic, and perhaps the Conservative Jews, the Bible is not taught as the Word of the God of Abraham, Isaac, and Jacob. Many, many Jewish people do not even believe in God. Years ago a survey revealed that about thirty-one percent of the Jewish people interviewed said they did not believe in God or they were not certain that God existed. This figure is no doubt much larger today. Multitudes of Jewish people are not taught that the Holy Scriptures are the inspired Word of God, and they are left to drift in the world system of materialism, good works, and personal accomplishments. The average Jewish person has no faith to sustain him or her as they walk through this life. They have no hope for life after death. They need our testimony of the reality of God almighty and the truthfulness of the Bible with its way to a personal relationship with the Lord through Messiah Jesus.

If you have a Jewish person who has married into your family, you will have a great opportunity to share your faith with him or her. However, though Jews marry outside of whatever their faith might be, most will still want to keep their Jewish heritage. They do not want to become Christians or Gentiles. Keep this in mind as you consider sharing what God means to you and what he has done for you in this life and for eternity. Your desire is that they experience God's great love, peace, guidance, and provision for sin to be forgiven through Messiah Jesus. In the third chapter of Galatians, it says that a Gentile who believes in Messiah Jesus is a descendant of Abraham by faith! After Jewish people have become believers, then church attendance will follow in time as the adjustment is made to their new faith.

If your granddaughter has married a Jewish man (let's call him David) and you seldom see them, take a tract or CD with you the next time you visit them. When you have the opportunity to talk with David alone, and after you have given him a big hug, say, "David, it is good to see you again. There is something that I want to share with you. I heard about a Jewish man (or met this Jewish man, as the case may be) and his relationship with the God of Israel that has given him great peace. He has peace from God even though his uncle Herman was murdered in the Holocaust at the Buchenwald Camp in Germany in WWII. He has been a Jewish Bible-believer for many years and shares his faith in God in what he has written and recorded on CDs. I have listened to this CD (or read this leaflet that he wrote) and want to get your opinion of it. I will leave it with you. The next time we get together, please let me know what you think of it. Thanks." If there is a table, just place the CD or tract on the table before you leave. If David is very friendly and you know he will accept the CD or tract, then hand it to him.

If he asks what the leaflet is about or what is on the CD, then share with him briefly: "Mr. Gruen has taken time to prepare this from his personal experience of his many years of knowing the God of Israel and the Bible. I think it would be best if you listen to the CD first and then we can discuss it. Okay?" It would be good for David to read the tract or listen to the CD when he has time to go over it carefully, or when he is alone. There should be no pressure. He would not be defensive if there is no one around before whom he could make negative remarks. It is possible that he will go over the material more than once as God speaks to his heart. Pray much for him after you leave and remember him daily in intercession before the Lord.

At a later time, as you have opportunity to speak with David about what he read or listened to, use Bible verses, prophecy, Isaiah 53, and other Scriptures to help him to put his faith in God, Messiah Jesus, and the Bible. Ask questions to see what progress he has made and whether or not he has an open heart. The Lord will guide you in every situation as you pray and depend on him. If he asks questions that you cannot answer, just say, "I don't have the answer to your question, but I will get it and share the answer with you soon." In this situation, please contact us by e-mail or letter, and you will have the answer in our reply. In over fifty-nine years of our sharing the Word of God with our Jewish people, we have been asked many, many questions that are upon the minds of Jews regarding the things of God. We are confident that we can help you, if you let us know the problem that has arisen during your witness.

> Withal praying also for us, that God would open unto us a door of utterance, to speak the mystery of Christ, for which I am also in bonds: That I may make it manifest, as I ought to speak.
>
> Colossians 4:3–4

2. NEIGHBORS

If you have Jewish neighbors, establish a good relationship with them by your love, kindness, and cheerful spirit. In your relationship with the Lord, you have salvation and the assurance of heaven when you die. Jews do not have this peace and joy. Material possessions can bring a degree of enjoyment and satisfaction, but the unbelievers' fear of death and the unknown future brings uncertainly to their lives. Acts of kindness go a long way to overcoming the apprehension Jews can have in their relationships with

Gentiles or Christians. Though you do not foster anti-Semitism, it is alive in the world today and Jews are aware of it. Your words and acts of love and care will show your neighbors that you do not hate them.

On one of our speaking trips in New Jersey, we met a dear Christian woman who was anxious to share her experience with us. She has a neighbor, an older Jewish woman, who had health problems. Since this Jewish woman lived alone and had no one to help her, it was difficult for her to care for herself and her home. The Christian woman offered to help her. She did the Jewish woman's meals, laundry, cleaned her house, and helped her with personal things. This went on for months. When the woman's health was restored and she could care for herself, she offered to pay the Christian for her help. God's servant said she would not accept any payment, for she had already received the greatest gift she could have from the Jewish people! She shared with this lost Jewish soul God's plan of salvation through Messiah Jesus. She said it was all Jewish! As a result of this testimony, the Jewish woman put her faith in Jesus and was wonderfully saved. Other Jews in the community also came to faith in Messiah Jesus! Acts of kindness open many doors to share the gospel and to see spiritual fruit in many Jewish lives.

If you have casual contact with Jewish neighbors, you can use this approach. When you see Sarah, tell her that you met (or know of) a Jewish man who has a wonderful relationship with the God of Israel: "He has put into a leaflet (or this CD) how he found real peace with God, himself and the future. I want to share what he wrote (or recorded) with you. Let me know what you think about it. I would like very much to have your opinion. Thanks. I have to go now, see you later." Hand the tract or CD to her or place it on a table if there is one near you and leave.

3. PROFESSIONAL AND BUSINESS PEOPLE

If your family physician is Jewish, you can share the gospel with him or her. After your visit is concluded, before leaving the doctor's office, offer the doctor either a tract or a CD. For a physician say, "Doctor, you have cared for me (or my family) for many years, and I am (we are) grateful for all you have done for me (us). Recently, I was given this leaflet (or CD) from a Jewish man who has a very special relationship to the God of Israel. His life is filled with peace, joy, security, and he has no fear of death for he knows he is going to heaven when he dies. Please read this (or listen to this) and let me know what you think about it the next time I see you." Place the tract or CD on his desk or table and leave. Do not hand it to the doctor, for then it can be refused for one reason or another. We have used this method of giving a tract and it does work. When you leave the CD or tract, you will have the joy of giving the gospel to a Jewish or Gentile physician. On your next visit, ask the doctor what he or she thought of the leaflet or CD. If the Lord is working in the doctor's heart, you may have the opportunity of sharing more of what you have learned in our studies on how to share your faith in Jesus.

The same approach can be used at a pharmacy. First, make certain to pick up your prescription and pay for it. Then, when no one else is at the counter and you can say a few words, use the same general approach that is used for a doctor. If the pharmacist is Jewish say, "Dr. Cohen, I have appreciated your care for our family's needs for prescriptions. I would like to leave something for you today that was given to me by a Jewish man who has a special relationship with the God of Israel. Look over it (or listen to it), and the next time I am in, let me know what you think about it." Place the tract or CD on the counter and leave. Do not hand it to him, for he can then refuse it.

At business or work, you can use the same approach as with physicians and pharmacists. Just say, "I have known you for sometime now and appreciate working with you. There is something that I would like to share with you that was given to me by a Jewish man who has a unique relationship with the God of Israel. Look it over (or listen to it) and let me know what you think about it during our lunchtime someday this week. I would value your opinion." In this situation, you might be able to place the CD or tract on a table or you might have to hand it to him. If you have to hand it to him, do so quickly and leave so that he does not have time to refuse it. Should your co-worker know you well, I doubt that he would refuse it. Be certain to ask about the tract or CD when you see him again later in the week.

4. COLLEGE AND UNIVERSITY STUDENTS

There is a tremendous opportunity for the Lord's people to share their faith in God, Messiah Jesus, and the Bible while on campus. Students are curious and have a mindset to learn and obtain knowledge. You will meet many atheists, agnostics, and students who have turned away from God and the Bible because of the hypocrisy they have seen in the lives of some religious people. Jews and Gentiles alike will have problems if they look at other people. They must be led to see what the Bible says for it is God's Word.

Christians should pray for opportunities to witness. You can use the same approach that you used with neighbors or professional people to give out CDs or tracts to students with whom you have become friendly. Pray for opportunities to read Isaiah 53 with Jewish students. Ask them, "Of whom does this speak?" They will most likely reply, "Jesus, but I don't believe in him." Tell them that Isaiah 53 was written by the Jewish man of God, Isaiah, about seven hundred years before Jesus lived here on earth. Ask your friend if you can go over the prophecy verse by verse to see just what it says. Other prophecies can be used in the same way. It is important to read as much Scripture as possible for as it says in Romans 10:17, "Faith comes by hearing, and hearing by the Word of God."

> The preparations of the heart in man, and the answer of the tongue is of the LORD...The wise in heart shall be called prudent: and the sweetness of the lips increaseth learning. The heart of the wise teacheth his mouth, and addeth learning to his lips.
>
> Proverbs 16:1, 21, 23

When you meet a Jewish student who has an interest in knowing God, you can go through the tract, "Have You Discovered the Principles for Personal Peace?" with him or her. Before you share this tract, review it yourself so that you are familiar with it. As you will see, the principle is given on the left page and a simple illustration on the right. The plan of the God of Israel for us to be forgiven of our sins is clearly presented. Take your time going through the principles. Do not rush. Be certain your inquirer understands what God is saying and then continue. Jews have been saved after going through this presentation of God's Word.

We have had the privilege of presenting our seminar on how to witness to Jews at a university in North Carolina where eighty Christian students and staff attended at the student center on campus. It was also our joy to give the seminar to seventy students and staff at a Campus Crusade for Christ meeting at Hampton Beach in New Hampshire. The students were grateful for the training that would help them share their faith with Jewish students at many colleges and universities across the United States. In our studies together you will have the same information that was given to the students plus much more. If you are a student, use the studies to help you share your faith in Jesus with Jews and Gentiles on campus. There are many needy young people on campus who need your testimony.

5. HIGH SCHOOL STUDENTS

In today's society, it is best if high school students look for opportunities to share their faith after school has dismissed for the day and they have left the school grounds. The Lord can give you an opening to speak for him while walking home or while waiting for a bus. A sixteen-year-old Christian girl was at a symposium where she met a sixteen-year-old unsaved Jewish teenager. They began talking about the subject of the meeting. The Christian girl led the conversation to talk about the Lord, for she has a burden to share God's Word with others. After a period of time during which the Jewish boy saw the genuine faith of this believer and her concern for him, he asked, "Why do Christians hate me?" This young man, in a city in Maryland, had somehow experienced anti-Semitism. It had affected him and his relationship to Gentiles whom he considered to be "Christians," but they were not true Bible-believers. With much patience, this dear Christian girl answered the questions that were asked. She helped this sixteen-year-old lost soul to understand that true Bible-believers love Jews and Gentiles and would never foster anti-Semitism of any kind. This Jewish young man was close to trusting Jesus as his Savior, but much prayer is needed to overcome family opposition. The Lord will use the faithful testimony of this Christian girl. We believe that someday he will put his trust in Messiah Jesus.

Look for opportunities to share your faith in Jesus. God will open doors for you to witness when you are burdened for lost souls and desire to lead them to redemption in Christ. Always leave gospel tracts or CDs with the young people with whom you share God's Word.

When you have someone who is interested in knowing just what you believe, suggest that you go through the booklet "Have You Discovered the Principles for Personal Peace?" Use the same procedure we suggested in the previous section on contacts with college and university students. If you do not have time to go through this tract, then leave a copy with your Jewish contact.

6. PUBLIC TRANSPORTATION AND TERMINALS

A number of years ago, George wrote the first copy of our tract, "Have You Discovered the Principles for Personal Peace?" The tract was in very large print. He took this new gospel literature with him on a trip from Philadelphia to New York City to show the tract to a Christian organization that might use it for a nationwide evangelistic outreach. As he was reading through the tract on the bus, a Jewish woman sitting across from him asked if he was a rabbi! She saw the Star of David on the cover. George said no but told her he was a Bible teacher. She had questions. It was his privilege to go through the booklet principle-by-principle to answer her questions and give her the way to be forgiven of sin according to the God of Israel. It was an unusual contact. Though she did not receive Jesus as her Savior on the bus, we believe we will see this Jewish woman in heaven.

Read this large-print tract in a restaurant or terminal where there might be Jewish people. Hold it up a little so someone sitting nearby will see the Star of David and possibly read some of the text. Pray for someone to see the booklet and then ask you questions. We never know where we will find a seeking heart. George has also used this booklet to witness to a family member who was not saved. Years later this family member did accept Jesus as his Savior, praise the Lord. If both husband and wife are with you, place the large-print tract on a table between them and go through it with them.

7. SPORTS ACTIVITIES—BASEBALL AND BASKETBALL

For many years, we used sports activities to invite Jewish young people to play on our team in a league. We had a Bible study after each game near the field or at a nearby home. The half-hour discussion from the Word of God was illustrated. The Lord blessed and souls were saved. Two of the Jewish young men who put their trust in Jesus said, "Why didn't someone tell us before that Jesus is our Jewish Messiah?" How would you answer that question?

There are countless lost souls who can be brought to faith in Jesus if we give them the opportunity to know what the Bible says!

8. COUNTY FAIRS—SHOPPING MALLS

These are good places to have a booth at which you give out gospel tracts, booklets, and even CDs. Many people will stop to look at the literature. As you talk with both Jews and Gentiles, there will be wonderful opportunities to share your faith in the Lord. We have given out thousands of gospel tracts over the years. We know the Lord has blessed his Word.

9. TRACT DISTRIBUTION

Various Christian groups have gone into the larger cities where there are many Jewish people and have given out tracts. Such efforts will find those who will take the tracts, but you will also find people who are antagonistic. Many good contacts have been made in these outreaches. The follow-up ministry has seen souls put their trust in Messiah Jesus.

Seek the Lord in prayer for his guidance to use you to give the gospel to lost souls. God has a place for you to serve him. You will rejoice as you walk with the Lord and are a faithful witness for Christ Jesus. It is wonderful to give his plan of salvation to souls and to see them believe and be redeemed.

Making It Personal

1. How can you share the gospel with a Jewish person who has married someone in your family?

2. Explain how you share a tract with a Jewish neighbor.

3. Is there a way that you can give God's Word to your doctor or pharmacist? Share how you can give the gospel to someone at work.

4. Is there a tract or booklet that can be given to a college or university student?

5. Can a witness be given to high school students? How?

6. Can you be a testimony in public transportation, terminals, or restaurants? Explain.

7. What other ways can we get the gospel to lost souls?

Additional Bible Verses for Study

*   Psalm 19:14
*   Proverbs 16:23–24
*   Acts 4:18–20
*   Romans 10:11
*   2 Timothy 1:7–10
*   1 Peter 4:11, 4:14, 4:16

Let's Witness to Jews

Understanding the Faith of Jewish People

PART A
Branches of Judaism and Their Beliefs

There are many different beliefs among Jewish people. The adherents to the largest groups are the Orthodox, Hasidic, Conservative, and Reform. Another movement is Reconstructionist that began in the 1900s. Multitudes of Jewish people have their names associated with one of these branches of Judaism but are not practicing or observant Jews. These Jewish people would be similar to Gentiles who attend church services on Easter and Christmas. There are multitudes of people who do not have a relationship to Almighty God our Heavenly Father and Messiah Jesus. Our hearts go out to these lost souls who live in great need to know the truth of the Holy Scriptures.

It is important that true Christians understand what the Bible, the Old Testament, means to Jewish people. The Orthodox and Hassidic for the most part will accept the Old Testament as coming from the God of Abraham, Isaac, and Jacob through the Jewish writers. Many Conservative Jews will also believe in the Bible, but individuals need to tell you what they believe. Do not assume that Jews believe the Bible is the Word of God. The Reform and Reconstructionist Jews do not accept the Bible as God's Word. Many Christians believe that Jews know a great deal about their Old Testament, but *that is not true.* You never need to be afraid of witnessing to a Jewish person because you think they know more about the Bible than you do. You will find most Jewish people have very little knowledge about the Holy Scriptures.

To many Jews, the Talmud is held on equal authority with the Bible. The Talmud is a collection of writings constituting the Jewish civil and religious law. The Talmud has two sections: the Mishnah and the Gemarah. Many Jewish people are taught that when God gave the written law to Moses on Mt. Sinai, God also gave an oral law to Moses. This oral law was handed down from generation to generation by word of mouth until it was put into writing around a d 200. These writings are called the Mishnah. The Rabbis then made commentaries on the Mishnah. These commentaries are called the Gemarah. The Mishnah and the Gemarah make up the many volumes in the Talmud. Many Jews know nothing or very little about the Talmud even as they have read very little of the Bible.

ORTHODOX JUDAISM

The adherents to this branch of the Jewish religion adhere to the traditions and rites of older Judaism. The holy days and holidays are observed as well as attire at Sabbath services. The Orthodox would endeavor to live by the *Siddur*, or Jewish prayer book. The Talmud would have great meaning to them and could be held on equal authority with the Bible. They should accept the Old Testament as God's Word, but this can vary among individuals. There are some Jews who will accept only the Torah, the five books of Moses, as the Word of God. They will attempt to keep the law of Moses as a means of pleasing God by their good works or deeds. They would not necessarily believe that the Tenach, consisting of the thirty-nine books in the Old Testament, are all God's Word. You will generally find a greater religious thought and activity among the Orthodox than in the other groups in Judaism. Orthodox Jews believe in the God of Israel. They support Israel and look forward to the rebuilding of the temple and the re-institution of the sacrifices. They believe that a human Messiah, similar to Moses, will come to bring peace to Israel. Their belief as to what happens after death can vary. Their services are held in synagogues.

As the Lord gives you the opportunity to become friendly with Jews of the Orthodox persuasion, your conversations will acquaint you with just what they believe. Ask sincere questions and most will answer them. Orthodox Jews, as well as Jews of any belief in Judaism, will not have the assurance of going to heaven when they die. All true Bible-believers possess great peace from the promises of God in the Bible. We will enter heaven after physical death. Always share this wonderful peace of the assurance of heaven by weaving it into your conversation. Unbelievers will question your belief about heaven, but this will give you the opportunity of sharing Bible verses that substantiate your faith. Many Orthodox Jews will give consideration to the Bible verses that you show them in the Old Testament because these are in their Bible.

> Brethren, my heart's desire and prayer to God for Israel is, that they might be saved. For I bear them record that they have a zeal of God, but not according to knowledge. For they being ignorant of God's righteousness, and going about to establish their own righteousness, have not submitted themselves unto the righteousness of God. For Christ [Messiah] is the end of the law for righteousness to every one that believeth.
>
> Romans 10:1–4

HASIDIC—HASIDIM

These Jewish people are very ardent in their relationship to God. Prayer is a central part of their lives and is motivated by their love for him. Prayer is very meaningful to the Hasid and should come from very deep feeling and concentration on the presence of God. They are very enthusiastic in their worship and for their faith in the God of Israel. The Hasidim conduct services of their own but consider themselves to be very Jewish.

CONSERVATIVE

This is a movement in Judaism that might accept the traditional forms of belief, worship, and rituals that are being observed by the Orthodox; however, Conservatives are free to modify them to make them relevant to modern living. These Jewish people can be flexible in their practices but are careful to maintain their "Jewishness." Conservatives do not leave tradition as the Reform and Reconstructionist have, but they might not practice as fully as the Orthodox. The practices of Conservative Judaism are in between the Orthodox and the Reform movement. They believe in God and the Holy Scriptures, though what is accepted might vary from individual to individual. Conservative Judaism began just before 1900 and developed as a Jewish faith not as strict as the Orthodox but not as liberal as the Reform movement that was active before the Conservative group began.

A Hebrew who is a Conservative Jew *might* be more interested in listening to your presentation of the Word of God than those who are of the Orthodox, Reform, or Constructionist persuasion. As with every contact, pray that the Spirit of God will give you wisdom and understanding as you share God's Word. Remember, it is always the Word of God that we present to inquirers.

REFORM

This is not a reformed group, but these Jewish people are of the Reform persuasion. There is no "ed" at the end of their name. This movement in Judaism began in the 1800s and has many adherents today. Years ago a rabbi of a Reform temple said that he did not believe in God. The congregation voted to keep him as their rabbi! They are foremost active in a brotherhood relationship to the people around them. They stress humanity and love for other people. Life is a matter of good deeds. Reform leadership changed the old *Siddur*, or prayer book to conform to their modernistic beliefs. They are not concerned with following what the Bible says about God, Messiah or the restoration of temple worship in Jerusalem with its sacrificial system for atonement. Reform Jews are taught that there is no resurrection of the dead. To the Reform Jew, there is no need to be concerned about sin, heaven, or hell. They do not believe in a personal Messiah but in a messianic era of peace that is brought about by human endeavors.

Reform Jewish people are taught that nations can achieve peace without God or the Messiah. Many radical changes were made in their days of worship and how their services are conducted. The word synagogue has been abandoned in favor of the temple as their place of worship. There have been some changes in the Reform movement in the twentieth century, but you will only learn what these Jewish people believe, or do not believe, as you have opportunity to talk with them.

In sharing the gospel with a Jewish person who attends a Reform temple, you will probably hear arguments similar to those of a Gentile atheist. It will be necessary for you to present the reasons you know the Bible is true.

It will take the Spirit of God moving upon the hearts of lost souls to stir them to seriously consider what you say. With Jews or Gentiles who are atheists or agnostics, we stress the need for everyone to be prepared to die! No one knows when death will come, for an accident can happen without warning. Bible-believers know what will happen the moment death comes. We will be in heaven! It is worth it to have such assurance. We know the promises given to us in the Bible, and we know the Bible is true and trustworthy. The difficulty many unbelievers have is that they have never talked to anyone who has told them what God has said to us in the Bible. We know and we must tell them!

> If any man speak, let him speak as the oracles of God; if any man minister, let him do it as of the ability which God giveth: that God in all things may be glorified through Jesus Christ, to whom be praise and dominion for ever and ever. Amen.
>
> 1 Peter 4:11

RECONSTRUCTIONIST

This movement in Judaism began in Pennsylvania in the 1900s. Those who follow this belief are mainly concerned with the here and now. They find no meaning in a personal God but believe in godliness or good deeds. They do not teach that there is an Almighty God for they reject the supernatural and miracles. Changes were made in the prayer book that were unacceptable to the Orthodox. The desire of the Reconstructionists is to make belief conform to modern thought. What will develop in the Reconstructionist movement in the future is unknown. We do know that all Jews and Gentiles need the gospel.

PART B
Holy days and Holidays

We will only consider the main holy days and holidays. There are many other such celebrations and observances, but these are not relevant to our study and would not be involved in your witness for the Lord.

PASSOVER

Passover, or *Pesach* (Hebrew, "pay-soch"), is the remembrance of the deliverance of the Jewish people from bondage and slavery as given in the book of Exodus, the second book of Moses. This holiday comes in March or April and is a seven-day celebration. The Passover celebration begins with the *Seder* (Hebrew, "say-der," which is the order of the ritual) that is conducted on the first and the second nights of Passover. This is a special service in Jewish homes for the entire family. A book called the *Haggadah* is read at the *Seder*. The *Haggadah* gives a narrative of the Exodus story and the

Seder ritual. Family members take part in the service that calls to remembrance God's deliverance of the Jewish people from bondage and all that was involved in their deliverance.

> … For even Christ [Messiah Jesus] our Passover is sacrificed for us.
>
> 1 Corinthians 5:7

There are many foods on the Passover table. There is a special Passover platter with (1) horseradish to symbolize the bitterness of slavery, (2) *haroset*, which is a mixture of nuts, apples, cinnamon, and wine, to symbolize the mortar out of which the Jewish people made bricks, (3) a roasted bone to remember the lamb that was slain, (4) roasted egg or eggs to remember the temple, or the two temples and the sacrifices offered there, (5) parsley to remember the hyssop that was dipped in the blood to apply to the doorpost, and (6) salt water to remember the tears shed in bondage. There are three *matzo* cakes that are placed in three compartments of a folded cloth that is called the *afikomen*. The middle *matzo* is broken and half of it is hidden to be brought back later in the service. Various meanings have been given for this part of the service. Jewish believers say this part of the service was added by believers to signify the death of Messiah Jesus as the middle *matzo* was broken. The half that was hidden was a reminder of his burial and later resurrection. It would be difficult for unsaved Jewish people to accept this; therefore, I do not use it in witnessing. There is also wine on the table that is partaken of four times to remember the promises of God to deliver the Hebrews from bondage. There is a separate place at the table with a cup that is for Elijah who is to come before Messiah comes. There is application for this for believers, but unbelievers would not accept this interpretation.

The entire service has to do with God's deliverance from bondage. One important part of the remembrance that God wanted Jews to include in the Passover was the blood of the lamb to remember the lamb that was slain for the Hebrews to be delivered from Egypt. Today there is only the shank bone of a lamb. Jesus the Messiah has provided for believers, both Jews and Gentiles, the type of the Passover Lamb by shedding his blood when he died to take upon himself the punishment due us for our sins. The Passover Lamb in Egypt died to bring deliverance to Jewish people from Egyptian bondage. Jesus died to deliver us from the bondage of sin. We read in John 1:29, "The next day John seeth Jesus coming unto him, and saith, Behold the Lamb of God, which taketh away the sin of the world." If people today do not have the Passover lamb in Messiah Jesus, they will not be forgiven of their sins according to God's Word. We read in Leviticus 17:11, "For the life of the flesh is in the blood: and I have given it to you upon the altar to make an atonement for your souls: for it is the blood that maketh an atonement for the soul." Isaiah 53 gives us the prophecy that Messiah would come to provide the blood of atonement for us to be forgiven of our sins. When we consider all of the prophecies that the God of Israel has given in the Old Testament, we know Messiah Jesus provided the blood of atonement for us.

Passover provides an excellent opportunity for you to witness to your Jewish friends. During Passover you might say to your neighbor: "Sarah, I know that this is your Passover. It has real meaning for me, too. When God delivered the Jewish people from bondage, he continued the line of Hebrews through whom God would send the Jewish Messiah to earth to provide the cleansing blood of atonement for both Jews and Gentiles. I have accepted the Jewish Messiah Jesus as my sin-bearer and have wonderful peace in my life from God. So you see, the Passover has real meaning in my life." The Lord will give you the words for every situation so you can be an effective witness for his glory.

ROSH HASHANAH—JEWISH NEW YEAR

The High Holy Days in the Jewish calendar include *Rosh Hashanah,* which is the Jewish New Year, and *Yom Kippur,* the Day of Atonement. To pious Jews, this is a time of awe as they seek God for the forgiveness of their sins. *Rosh Hashanah* comes first and usually is in September. It begins with the blowing of the ram's horn that ushers in a ten-day period when observing Jews search their hearts for the sins they have committed against God during the past year. There are special services in the synagogue for Jews to seek God.

For Jews who are not religious, this will be a family

time to begin another New Year. They will not deal with sin and their relationship to God, for they are not concerned about God and his plan of redemption for Jews and Gentiles.

You can send your Jewish friends a card to wish them a Happy New Year. There are sections for these cards in card stores. They will appreciate your thoughtfulness. Sometimes a good tract that is written for Jewish people can be included as the Lord leads. You might add a note with the tract to say that this leaflet was given to you by a Jewish man (if it is one of our tracts) and it has to do with God's atonement and *Yom Kippur.*

YOM KIPPUR—THE DAY OF ATONEMENT

The ten days of heart-searching and repentance culminate with the Day of Atonement. There are meetings in the synagogue, beginning on the eve of *Yom Kippur,* for Jewish people to seek God for the forgiveness of their sins. When the Jewish temple was still in Jerusalem, animal sacrifices for the blood of atonement were offered there to obtain God's forgiveness as God required on the Day of Atonement in Leviticus 16. After the temple was destroyed in a d 70, there was no place to offer the blood of atonement commanded by the God of Israel in the law of Moses. In place of the blood of atonement, Rabbis substituted the present way for Jews to seek God for atonement. Jewish people are required to do three things on the Day of Atonement in order to be forgiven of their sins: (1) confess their sin and ask for God's forgiveness,

(2) fast for twenty-four hours, and (3) give gifts to their place of worship. Much Scripture is read in the services. Today, not everyone adheres to all three requirements.

> Thy word is true from the beginning: and every one of thy righteous judgments endureth for ever.
>
> Psalm 119:160

There is no blood of atonement in today's Jewish worship; therefore, there is no forgiveness of sin. Almighty God has given his Word in the Bible as to what Jews and Gentiles are to believe to be cleansed of sin and experience his peace. Just before the Jewish temple was destroyed in a d 70, God sent Messiah Jesus to die in a d 32–33 to provide the once-for-all-time blood of atonement so all people would have access to the cleansing blood. In Colossians 1:12–14 we read,

> Giving thanks unto the Father, which hath made us meet to be partakers of the inheritance of the saints in light: Who hath delivered us from the power of darkness, and hath translated us into the kingdom of his dear Son: In whom we have redemption through his blood, even the forgiveness of sins.

We read in Romans 5:8–9, 5:11,

> But God commendeth his love toward us, in that, while we were yet sinners, Christ [Messiah] died

for us. Much more then, being now justified by his blood, we shall be saved from wrath through him ... And not only so, but we also joy in God through our LORD Jesus Christ [Messiah], by whom we have now received the atonement.

We have this wonderful message to share with Jewish people and Gentiles. The blood of atonement that God demanded for people to be forgiven of their sins is found today in Messiah Jesus. Salvation is made personal as we ask God to forgive us of our sins and we put our faith in Jesus as our atonement.

As the Spirit of God leads you, the week after Yom Kippur is a good time to talk with your Jewish friend. Use this approach: "David, I know that you have just come through your High Holy Days and the Day of Atonement. You have sought God for his forgiveness of your sins of the past year and have asked him to inscribe your name in God's Book of Life. Do you truly know now that God has forgiven you of your sins? Do you have perfect assurance that when you die you will go to heaven for eternity? I know in my own life that through the Bible and Messiah I have found the atonement and forgiveness of my sins. I know that someday, when I die, I will be in heaven with the God of Israel for eternity. I was wondering if you have this same assurance?" As David asks questions, you should have a good opportunity to share your faith in Messiah Jesus. Do not force anything; let the conversation flow naturally.

HANUKKAH—FESTIVAL OF DEDICATION AND LIGHTS

This is a joyous holiday for Jewish people. It is celebrated in December. It remembers the victory led by the Jewish Judah Maccabeus over the army of Antiochus IV, King of Syria. The Jewish temple in Jerusalem had been captured and made into a pagan shrine. Antiochus wanted to destroy the Jewish religion with all of its practices. God raised up Maccabeus to lead the Jews to victory in a three-year war from 168 to 165 bc. When Jerusalem was retaken, the temple was cleansed, rededicated, and the temple worship restored. This was another God-given victory to the descendants of Abraham.

The festival of lights is celebrated for eight days. The *Hanukkah Menorah* has eight candles to represent these days with a new candle being lit every day. There is one candle that is elevated above the rest that is called the Servant. This candle is lit first and from it all of the other candles get their light. This is interesting for Bible-believers, for Messiah Jesus is the Servant of God who gives light to all who trust in him.

Hanukkah has meaning for true Christians. You can share these thoughts with your Jewish friends. In this God-given victory over Antiochus, God preserved Judaism for us along with the Jewish Scriptures, the Old Testament. Without this victory, we would not have known Messiah Jesus and would not have had the records to prove he was a descendant of King David on his human side. We would not have had the prophecies in the Old Testament Scriptures to prove Jesus is the Jewish Messiah. The records were preserved that make clear to us that we have the redeeming blood of atonement in Jesus. Praise the Lord!

Making It Personal

1. What books are in the Jewish Bible? What is the Jewish Talmud?

2. What are Orthodox Jews? What do they believe?

3. What are Hasidic Jews? What is their faith?

4. Compare Conservative Judaism to the Orthodox and Hasidic.

5. What do we know about Reform Judaism?

6. What do Jews of the Reconstructionist faith believe?

7. Briefly explain the Jewish holy days and holidays of Passover, New Year, Day of Atonement, and *Hanukkah*. How can we witness to Jews during these special days?

Additional Bible Verses for Study

*   Exodus 12:3–14
*   Exodus 15:1–11

- Leviticus 16:2–6, 16:14–16, 16:29–30
- Acts 4:12
- Hebrews 9:11–12
- Hebrews 10:9–10, 10:12
- Hebrews 12:1–2

Relationships with New Jewish Believers

Jewish people, who put their trust in Jesus as their Messiah and Savior, usually will face opposition to their new relationship to God and Jesus. Family, relatives, and friends can be very vocal and harsh in their condemnation of one in their family who has trusted in the Lord. Parents and others will endeavor to talk the new believer out of his or her faith, or they might use enticements to draw their family member away from Jesus. One Jewish young man was offered a new automobile if he would give up his faith in Jesus. He did not accept the offer and remained true to his new life in the Lord. Orthodox and Hasidic Jews will offer the most vehement opposition. The more liberal the Jewish family is in their Judaism, the less antagonistic they might be; however, all unsaved Jews might stand against a Jewish person believing in Jesus. The reason for this is obvious. Jewish people have been persecuted by so-called Christians and have suffered abuse by people who claim to believe in Jesus but are not true Bible-believers. When a family member shares his or her new faith in Jesus, others in the Jewish household will believe that their loved one has become one with the persecutors of the Jewish people. Of course, this is not true. It will take time for the family to understand the truth, if they are willing to listen.

Jews have two Hebrew words that they use to identify Jewish people who have put their faith in Jesus. *Meshuginah*—crazy—for a Jew who believes in Jesus must be crazy, and *Meshumad*—apostate—abandoning their Jewish faith. The new believer must be assured that both expressions certainly do not apply to a believer in Messiah Jesus. A Jew is not crazy to believe in what the Almighty God of Israel has said that Jews must believe. Our faith is in the Word of God in the Bible that was given to us through the Jewish prophets and followers of the God of Israel. Jews who are believers in God's Judaism are certainly not apostate, for they now have faith in the God of the Bible and what God expects of every Jew and Gentile. The new Jewish believer's faith rests upon the foundation of the Bible that has been given to us by the true and living God.

Much love and support must be shown to new Jewish believers. They will need guidance from God's Word to show God's love for their family, relatives, and friends. They will need to understand why their family opposes their faith in Jesus. The problem of anti-Semitism must be explained as to who actually is responsible for it. No true Bible-believers will foster anti-Semitism. *True* Christians will live by Genesis 12:1–3 and never speak against the Jewish people. God will bless those who bless the Jews and curse those who curse the Jewish people.

> And ye shall know the truth, and the truth shall make you free.
>
> John 8:32

New Jewish believers must be encouraged to love their families and friends who oppose their faith in Jesus. If they are living at home, their actions must show their new love for God that has changed their lives. This will go a long way to helping their parents, grandparents, and other family members to understand what accepting Messiah Jesus has done in their lives. It will not be easy, but the Lord will see them through to a victorious life as they pray, trust, and obey the Bible admonitions concerning family relationships.

Parents often want their teenagers who have put their trust in Messiah Jesus to visit their rabbi. They expect their rabbi to talk the new believer out of his or her faith in Jesus. If the new believer has been truly grounded in the prophecies about Jesus in Isaiah 53 and other Scriptures, there should be no difficulty in the visit. One of the Jewish young men who put his trust in the Lord through our youth program went to see the family rabbi at the insistence of his Orthodox parents. Abe shared his faith in the Jewish Messiah from Isaiah 53 and why he put his trust in Jesus. The rabbi had no rebuttal for Abe's presentation but asked Abe to see another religious teacher. Abe did so and shared again the Word of God from the Bible. After another visit to a third religious leader, no one bothered Abe again.

The new believers are certain to hear emotional appeals to give up their faith in Jesus. We must encourage them to be faithful to what the God of Israel says in his Word. New believers, Jewish or Gentile, must be grounded in the Holy Scriptures. Our foundation for faith is not emotional but factual! The Bible is true!

In our ministry with Jewish young people, we saw many put their faith in the Bible and accept Jesus as their Messiah and Savior. We then encouraged them to have daily Bible reading and prayer. We also had evening Bible studies and prayer meetings with them. Such meetings were good times to answer their questions. They had many questions! Much time was also spent on the telephone as the faith of the new believers was challenged. Be prepared to spend time to help new Jewish believers grow in grace and have the knowledge they need to share their faith with others. Your time spent in this way will certainly be worth it! You will be amazed at the faith and desire to witness that you will see in new Jewish believers.

If the Jewish believer wants to attend Jewish holiday meetings with the family, it should not be harmful, as long as the believer is strong in his or her faith in Messiah Jesus. Jewish heritage can be maintained as long as it does not add works to grace for salvation.

Do not rush a Jewish believer to attend church. Some will be ready to go with you soon after their salvation while others will take more time. If you have a cross in the sanctuary, and most churches do, give a brief explanation for it. Just say, "You will notice in our meeting place that there is a cross. It is to remind believers of the blood of atonement that Messiah Jesus shed for us when he died to take the judgment due us for our sins." Hopefully, the Jewish person will feel at home in the midst of a group of Gentile Christians. Pray that those who attend the service will be friendly. You might have to explain the music or songs, but this should not be a problem. Tell him or her to pass the offering plate to you. Pray for the Holy Spirit to watch over the new Jewish believer. Make the visit to church be a good one.

Should there be any mention of a baptismal service, just say that this can be discussed in the months ahead. Briefly, baptism is an outward expression of the inward work of God in the life of the believer.

Through the years, we have answered many questions from family members and friends that objected to someone in the family placing his or her faith in Messiah Jesus. We share a number of these questions and answers with you so you will be prepared to assist the new child of God. Space does not permit us to give detailed answers, but you will have sufficient information to reply.

> Ye therefore, beloved, seeing ye know these things before, beware lest ye also, being led away with the error of the wicked, fall from your own steadfastness. But grow in grace, and in the knowledge of our Lord and Savior Jesus Christ [Messiah] …
>
> 2 Peter 3:17–18

FAMILY ARGUMENTS AGAINST NEW JEWISH BELIEVERS

1. *"You will become a Goy." Goy* is a Gentile. They are saying that when a Jew accepts Jesus, he or she is no longer a Jew but is a Gentile. There is nothing in the Jewish Bible that says a Jew who believes in Messiah Jesus is no longer Jewish. Judaism might teach this, but it is not what God says. In fact, believers usually are more Jewish than before! They believe in the God of Abraham. They accept the entire Bible as the Word of the God of Israel. They believe in what God says in the Bible about heaven, hell, sin, how to be forgiven of sin, love, peace, relationships with other people, and in living a life that is pleasing to Almighty God.

2. *"You don't know enough. Learn your own religion first. Our rabbi can explain these things."* The new believer has learned much about God, Messiah, the Bible, and how to have peace with God in this life and for eternity in heaven. The believer knows that sin has been forgiven and there is now joy in living. The Bible is a living book from God that gives meaning and purpose to life and eternity. These truths are not taught in Judaism. The rabbi does not have the answers to life, death, and eternity.

3. *"Needing God is a crutch; it shows weakness of character. You should rely on yourself."* We are sinners and cannot rid ourselves of our sins by good deeds. No human effort can give a person a right relationship to God. The Jewish man of God, Ezekiel, recorded this in the Bible in Ezekiel

33:11–13. A right relationship to God is not a crutch; it is a necessity. Food is not a crutch. A car is not a crutch. A house is not a crutch. These are necessary as is a right relationship to the God who created us. We cannot save ourselves from our sins, only God can. The Bible is our roadmap for this life and for eternity. We all need God and the Bible; without them, we perish.

4. "How can we have a personal relationship with God? We can't see him or know about him." We can definitely know God through the Bible. People do not know God for they do not read the Holy Scriptures. The only book that reveals God is the Bible. People will be amazed at the knowledge they will gain about Almighty God when they read his revelation about himself in the Bible.

5. "This is all ridiculous." No, it is very rational. As we learn what the Bible says, the truth of the Holy Scriptures makes sense, and it is really terrific! Hebrews 4:12, "For the Word of God is quick, and powerful, and sharper than any two edged sword … and is a discerner of the thoughts and intents of the heart." Psalm 119:105, "Thy [God's] word is a lamp unto my feet, and a light unto my path." The Bible, God's Word, makes life worth living and prepares us for life after death in heaven. This is not ridiculous!

> There is a way that seemeth right unto a man, but the end thereof are the ways of death.
>
> Proverbs 16:25

6. "We do not need the blood sacrifices today. Back then God was trying to get the Jewish people away from worshipping idols and barbarianism." The only record we have of the history of our Jewish people is given to us in the books of Moses, Genesis through Deuteronomy, as well as all of the books of the Jewish Bible or the Old Testament. The God of Israel spoke through Moses to tell us why we needed the blood of atonement to be forgiven of our sin and how we were to obtain it. This is clearly given in the third book of Moses, Leviticus chapters 5 and 16. We human beings certainly cannot presume to tell the Almighty God of Israel why he gave the instructions that he did. We are his creation and are to obey what God has given to us in the Bible regarding the blood of atonement. We know from the Jewish Bible that today the Jewish atonement is found in the Messiah as it is recorded for us in Isaiah 53.

7. "People are not inherently bad or sinful, just human. Look at all of the good things that people do." People have done good things, but all have still sinned according to God's Word in the Bible. In the Old Testament, the Jewish Bible, we read in Ecclesiastes 7:20, "For there is not a just [good] man upon earth, that doeth good, and sinneth not." Yes, there are good people, but *all* people have sinned. Sin must be forgiven according to God's instructions. In Psalm 51, King David of Israel tells us that we all sin and need God's forgiveness.

8. "I thought you were an intelligent person. How can you be so stupid to believe this?" The enemy of our souls always

George and Jean Gruen

plays on the ego. People of great learning believe the Bible and trust in God and his plan for our lives. The great Jewish men in the Bible, Abraham, Moses, Joseph, King David, King Solomon, Isaiah, and many, many others gave to us the history of the Hebrew people and all that the God of Israel has given to the world through them. We are not going to reject God's Word and accept what people have taught. In our Bible studies, there was a Jewish young man who put his trust in Messiah Jesus. He was very educated and held a position as a research chemist. His father and mother were proud of their *intelligent son.* When they heard of his faith in Messiah Jesus, he found a note under his pillow stating that his parents were so disappointed in his lack of intelligence! How sad it is when prejudice clouds the minds of people and hinders them from an examination of the facts when it comes to God, Messiah Jesus, and the Bible.

> Therefore hell [*Sheol*] hath enlarged herself, and opened her mouth without measure: and their glory, and their multitude, and their pomp, and he that rejoiceth, shall descend into it.
>
> Isaiah 5:14

9. *"Heaven and hell are just fictitious terms used in the Bible."* The Bible is all true, not just the parts that some people want to accept. Heaven and hell are very real places that the Word of God describes in detail in the Bible.

10.   "The Bible is a good book, but it is not meant to be taken literally." Who said that it is not to be taken literally? Of course it must be taken literally, for we know it is the word of Almighty God. Fulfilled prophecy, the discoveries of archeologists and your personal experience are the foundation stones of knowing the Bible is the Word of God.

11.   "If you believe in this, keep your opinions to yourself. You should not try to convert other people. Jews don't proselytize." The Judaism that is in the Bible did try to bring people to its faith. We read in Psalm 51:12–13, "Restore unto me the joy of thy salvation; and uphold me with thy free spirit. Then will I teach transgressors thy ways; and sinners shall be converted unto thee [God]." These are the words of God through King David of Israel. Since it was good enough for King David, one of the greatest Jews who ever lived, to say these words, then it is good enough for us and other Jews to use them! In the Bible to be converted is to change from living in sin to living for God in his will. Some versions for "converted" say, "be brought back to," which has the same general meaning. Since sin takes the sinner away from God, the sinner should be taught God's way for sinners to be forgiven and be brought back to God's way. The Bible is filled with instructions for believers to share God's Word with lost souls. In Isaiah 6:8–9 we read, "Also I heard the voice of the Lord, saying, Whom shall I send, and who will go for us? Then said I, Here am I; send me [Isaiah, the Jewish man of God]. And he [God] said, Go, and tell this people …" The God of

Israel told Isaiah to go and speak his word to the Jewish people. If you have read the book of Isaiah in the Jewish Holy Scriptures, then you know that Isaiah was a prophet of God to the children of Israel. We also are to take God's plan of salvation to the Jewish people. All Christians will find this commission from God given in Romans 1:16.

12. *"Jews don't talk about Christ and say he is Lord or God."* It is true that Jewish people do not refer to Jesus as Lord, for they only believe in one God, if they actually do believe in God. When we say Lord Jesus, we do say that Jesus is God, and we should. In our study of the Godhead, we found that in the Old Testament, Messiah is one in the Godhead. Then Messiah would come to earth and take on human form in Jesus by the Virgin Birth. This makes Jesus the Son of God and Messiah Jesus. Use the Bible verses in this study when you have the opportunity to share what the Bible says about the Godhead.

> The way of life is above to the wise, that he may depart from hell [*Sheol*] beneath.
>
> Proverbs 15:24

13. *"I don't have to read the literature you gave me because I have seen it before."* It is doubtful that most Jewish people have been given a Bible tract that has been written for Jews. The believer might then ask his Jewish parents, who said they have seen this before, to show him the leaflet. He could then make comment on it. If they discarded

it, then he could offer them the tract he had and ask for their opinion of it. He might say, "Your opinion would be appreciated." Use our tracts "Peace in These Times" or "Have You Discovered the Principles for Personal Peace?" which have been specifically written for Jewish people. Pray silently before offering the tract.

14. *"It's wrong for a Jew to believe in Jesus."* In the teaching of Judaism today, it is not acceptable for a Jewish person to believe in Jesus; however, this is not what the God of Israel says in his Holy Scriptures, the Bible. God-given prophecy through the Jewish men of God in the Old Testament, or the Jewish Bible, definitely reveals to us who the Messiah would be when he would come to earth the first time to provide the atonement for us. Isaiah 53 clearly gives to us a picture of the Messiah. Other prophecies identify the Messiah so we would not misunderstand what God was doing for us. When these prophecies are studied, we know beyond any doubt that Jesus is our promised Jewish Messiah. The problem that Jewish people face is that they have teachers who will not examine the facts and believe the truth. Their doctrines of the past are hard to give up, even in the face of absolute truth. Accepting Messiah Jesus is the will of the God of Abraham, Isaac, and Jacob for Jews and all people. If people do not accept Messiah Jesus as their sin-bearer, they have no blood of atonement and no forgiveness for their sins according to the requirements of the God of Israel.

15. *"What about the Christian woman who became a Jew?"* There are Gentile men and women who, in order to marry Jews, convert to Judaism. These people, for the most part, would not be true, Bible-believing Christians. We are certain that there are some Bible-believers who do marry unsaved Jewish people. They hope that they will be able to show the unbelieving spouse the way of salvation in Jesus and lead them to faith in him.

16. *"Beside the Bible, you should read…"* There are books today on religion and philosophy that will not meet the spiritual need of sinful hearts. Our purpose in sharing God's Word with Jews and Gentiles is to give them the opportunity to know how their sins can be forgiven, and how they can have absolute assurance of going to heaven when they die. The Bible, the Word of Almighty God, is the only book that gives men and women, Jews and Gentiles, this perfect peace concerning eternity. The Holy Scriptures also equip us to live in this life in peace, joy, guidance, provision, fulfillment, and fellowship with God. Only trusting God's Word can give such a life!

17. *"Nobody is as happy as you say these people are."* We live in a society where there is much sorrow, illness, distress, and problems. When a Bible-believer experiences God's forgiveness of sin in his or her life, it brings real peace and joy. Through trusting all of the promises of God in the Bible for believers, there is tremendous happiness and a great smile to be shared with people! Such joy can be experienced by all Jews and Gentiles who put their faith in Messiah Jesus. Bible-believers are to live lives before unbelievers that will cause them to seek the life we have in the Lord.

18. "These are modern times, much of the Bible is outdated. God's laws were made to be changed." This is not true. The Bible is as relevant today as it was thousands of years ago. It is not outdated. The way of atonement has changed and is now through Messiah and not at the Jewish temple in Jerusalem. God knew the temple would be destroyed in a d 70, and he foretold, by the Jewish prophets, that Messiah Jesus would come to provide the blood of atonement before the temple would be destroyed. We are also forgiven of our sins by faith in Messiah Jesus' atonement and not by the works of the law. Good deeds do not atone for our sins. Jews and Gentiles, who trust the Bible's way to be right with God, are living in peace and joy. Those who do not trust in the way of salvation in Messiah Jesus do not have real peace in this life and they have no answer for what happens after death.

19. "People can twist the Bible to say anything." It is possible for people to say the Bible says something when it does not say it. God expects us, as intelligent people, to read for ourselves and make a judgment on the issue under discussion. In so doing, we must be honest and not avoid the truth. The Bible says in John 8:32, "Ye shall know the truth, and the truth shall make you free." When a person trusts what the Bible says, then the life of that individual will reflect the truth that is presented in the Holy Scriptures. To illustrate, we read in the Old Testament in Proverbs 3:5–6, "Trust in the LORD with all thine heart; and lean not unto thine own understanding. In all thy ways acknowledge him, and he shall direct thy paths." This is true! When we trust God and not our own understanding, and we commit our way to him, God will direct the path we should take and it will be terrific!

In the New Testament we read in Philippians 4:6–7, "Be careful [anxious or fearful] for nothing; but in everything by prayer and supplication with thanksgiving let your requests be made known unto God. And the peace of God, which passeth all understanding, shall keep your hearts and minds through Christ Jesus." This promise from God tells us that we are not to worry about anything, but we are to bring every situation to the Lord in earnest prayer. We are to thank the Lord for the answer even before it comes—that is faith! When we do, we will have such great peace that people will not understand it. The peace of God by his Spirit will keep our emotions and intellect under control. What wonderful promises from God. The Lord keeps his promises to us. We can testify that this has happened in our lives again and again. We praise the Lord for all the promises he has given to us.

20. *"If I accept Jesus as my Messiah and Redeemer, I then say that my parents/grandparents who did not accept Jesus are in hell. This is hard for me to accept."* We do not know if your parents/grandparents were Jewish Bible-believers. They might have been but never told anyone in the family. George Gruen had grandparents on his father's side who were very Orthodox Jews in Europe in the early 1900s. His grandfather, Paul Gruen, became the disciple of Rabbi Joseph Babat, the most renowned rabbi of Poland. As a student, Paul knew Hebrew well. A younger

Jewish man, who was a Bible-believer, challenged Paul to study Old Testament prophecy. Mr. Gruen had not seen these prophecies before. After much study, he knew that Jesus was the Jewish Messiah and accepted him. Paul was afraid to tell his wife of his faith in Jesus, for it would destroy the family. One day he got up courage and began to tell her. To his great surprise, Emilie said, *"I am a believer, too!"* She was afraid to tell him of her faith in Jesus. They rejoiced together! If Paul had died before he told his wife, she would have thought he died as an unbeliever. If she had died, he would have felt the same way. *There are Jewish people who believe in Jesus who have not told anyone in their family of their faith in Jesus for fear of severe opposition, especially in Orthodox or Hasidic homes.* There are times when we do not know if a loved one was a believer or not. There are people who, when near death, have put their faith in Messiah Jesus. Only God knows. You can share this with Jews who wonder about loved ones who have died.

Let us be faithful in sharing God's plan of redemption with unbelievers so that they might have the opportunity to put their trust in Messiah Jesus before it is too late.

> Being confident of this very thing, that he which hath begun a good work in you will perform it until the day of Jesus Christ.
>
> Philippians 1:6

Making It Personal

1. Will new Jewish believers in Jesus suffer persecution because of their faith? Who will foster this persecution? Why?

2. How can persecution and opposition be overcome?

3. How can new believers grow in grace? What are two essentials for their new life in Jesus?

4. What about church attendance? Small group meetings? Should they attend Jewish religious services and holidays? What will you say to a new believer as you bring him/her to your church?

5. Who is a Goy? What does this mean to a Jewish believer?

6. What are some family arguments against new believers?

Additional Bible Verses for Study

- Romans 5:7–11, 11:11–14, 11:30–31
- 2 Corinthians 5:8–10, 5:14–15, 5:17–18
- Ephesians 6:10–19
- Hebrews 9:11–12, 9:14, 9:19–28, 10:19–24

Epilogue

It has been our desire to give a basic understanding of how you can share your faith in Jesus. It is an exciting journey to walk with the Lord and to please him by giving the gospel to Jews and Gentiles.

Let's Witness to Jews has provided the information you need to step out in faith for Christ to be his ambassador to needy hearts. You are never alone in this task. The Spirit of God within you will go before you, work through you, sustain you in every situation, and make you a blessing. It might not be comfortable for you to share your faith when you first launch out for the Lord. As you determine to tell others about Jesus, witnessing will become a normal part of living. You will enjoy it! Christians have the awesome privilege of serving the Almighty God of creation. How wonderful!

Prayer, patience, and perseverance in sharing the Word of God will make you a faithful, joyful Christian. You can do it! Ask God to lead you to someone this week with whom you can talk about Jesus.

Don't hesitate to contact us if you need help in any aspect of sharing your faith. Be certain to go to our website www.sharinggodstruth.org to obtain our tracts and CDs that will assist you in your outreach for the Lord. The Lord bless you.

Appendix

ANSWERS TO QUESTIONS

God's Gift—Our Responsibility

1. Is prayer and living the Christian life sufficient for a believer to see a lost soul come to faith in Jesus for salvation? Explain your answer.

    Answer: People only become Christians by believing the gospel, confessing their sins to God, and accepting Christ Jesus as their sin-bearer. If they do not hear or read the gospel message of salvation, they will not be saved. A believer who lives the Christian life without sharing the gospel will not see souls saved.

2. Does God expect all Christians to audibly share their faith in Jesus? Why?

    Answer: Yes, for without an audible witness, or the gospel given in tract form, souls will not know how to be saved. There is no place in the Bible where the Lord exempts any Bible-believer from being a witness for Jesus.

3. How can a Christian learn to witness to Jews?

    Answer: Christians can learn how to witness to Jewish people by attending seminars on Jewish evangelism or by a book such as this one. After a careful study of the materials in this book, believers will be prepared to share their faith in Jesus with Jewish people. The fears that keep the Lord's people from witnessing will be alleviated. They can be confident that the Lord will use their testimony.

4. Do believers witness to Jews the same way and with the same methods and terminology as they do to Gentiles? Why?

   Answer: Because of what Jews have suffered at the hands of so-called Christians in the name of Christ Jesus, it is necessary to share the Word of God by using different terminology and methods so Jews can understand and be saved.

5. Do you feel confident to share your faith with your Jewish friends? Practice sharing your faith now with someone in your group or have a friend listen to you.

   Answer: If you do not feel confident to witness to Jewish people, you will know how to share your faith with Jews after you complete this study. As you learn what to say, what not to say, how to use prophecy and answer questions, the Lord will use your testimony. You will have great joy in witnessing for Jesus. Break your group into two's and encourage them to take 5 minutes each in practicing the words they will use when they meet a Jewish person.

6. Are only missionaries, pastors, and full-time Christian workers supposed to witness to Jewish and

Gentile people? Is this found in the Holy Scriptures? Where?

Answer: The Lord commands all of his children to share their faith with the Jewish people. This privilege is not limited to those in full-time service. Every Christian must witness to the Jewish people by word or literature if we are to be faithful to the Lord's command to give Jews the opportunity to know the gospel. That we are all to witness is found in many places in the Holy Scriptures. One example would be Matthew 28:19, "Go ye therefore, and teach all nations, baptizing them in the name of the Father, and of the Son, and of the Holy Ghost." Jesus gave each one of us a direct command–GO! He didn't say GO to only those who are in full-time service but rather GO to each one of us.

7. If no one shared the gospel with you, would you have salvation and the assurance that you are going to heaven when you die?

Answer: If the gospel had not been shared with you by your mother, father, brother, sister, relative, pastor, Sunday school teacher, TV or radio preacher, friend, or someone else, you would not be saved today. Someone had to tell you how to know Jesus as your Savior. It is now the Lord's will for you to tell others how to be saved.

Terminology when Witnessing

1. Do the experiences that unsaved Jews have been through need to be considered as we share the gospel? How have these experiences affected Jews?

   Answer: Jewish people have suffered greatly by open and subtle anti-Semitism. The persecution and death they endured during the crusades, the Spanish Inquisition, the Holocaust, and untold persecution must be considered as you witness to Jews. By your love, compassion, care, and sharing you can begin to break down prejudice and open the way to share God's plan of redemption through Messiah Jesus. It will take time.

2. Do you witness to Jews the same as Gentiles? Share the differences or similarities.

   Answer: Gentiles have not suffered at the hands of so-called Christians and the church, and they do not have the same problems as Jews do when considering Jesus. Hypocrisy in the lives of people who profess to be Christians, but are not, is a hindrance to all unbelievers. God can overcome difficulties as we share his love. Review words such as Christian vs Bible-believer and Old-Testament vs Jewish Holy Scriptures.

3. Should we speak of the Lord Jesus Christ in our sharing with Jewish people? What problem might hinder your witness? When speaking of Christ Jesus, it would be better to use what words?

Answer: Jews believe in only one God. When we say Lord Jesus, we say to Jewish people that we believe in two Gods. To them, Lord means God. It is best to say Messiah Jesus until you have explained the Godhead from the Old Testament.

4. Should we use the term Christian with Jews? If not, why not, and what should we call ourselves?

   Answer: Jewish people believe that Christians hate them and Christians are responsible for much of the suffering that Jews have endured. Rather than calling yourself a Christian, call yourself a Bible-believer. God gave us the Bible and trusting it brings peace and joy. We share the Bible and not a religion.

5. How do Jews feel about the church? How do we explain the church to inquirers?

   Answer: If you speak about church, it can bring to the Jewish mind thoughts of the Spanish Inquisition where the church told Jews to convert and join the church or die. Thousands of Jewish people were put to death when they refused to go to that church. Rather than saying you go to church, just say you attend meetings where you learn about God and the Bible.

6. We rejoice in the cross on which Christ Jesus died for our sins to be forgiven. Do Jewish people have any problem with talking about the cross? Why? If so, what else can we say rather than the cross?

Answer: Yes, Jewish people have a tremendous problem talking about or seeing the cross. When the Crusaders marched through Europe to the Holy Land to free Jerusalem from its inhabitants, they murdered Jews and destroyed Jewish communities along the way. In Jerusalem they herded Jewish men, women, and children into the big synagogue and burned it to the ground. The Jews were murdered. The crusaders sang Christian songs as they marched around the burning synagogue. On their lances and tunics, the crusaders had the symbol of the cross. Jews still remember. Rather than say cross, just say the place where Messiah Jesus died to provide the blood of atonement for people to be forgiven of their sins.

7. Why should you not use the word convert or converted when sharing God's plan for our lives? What Scripture in the Old Testament explains converting?

Answer: In the Spanish Inquisition, Jews were told to convert from Judaism to the church or they would be put to death. To Jews, to convert is to change from being Jewish to being a Christian or a Gentile. If the subject of converting comes up, say you believe in converting as King David of Israel did in Psalm 51. King David said that converting is changing from a life of sin to a life of being forgiven of our sins by God and living for Him. It was good for King David of Israel; it is good for me!

8. What words can best describe the Old Testament when talking with Jews? Should you say New Testament?

Answer: You can refer to the Old Testament as the Jewish Bible or Jewish Holy Scriptures. You can also say that the God of Israel spoke to Jewish men who trusted in him and recorded his Word. We have this recorded Word of God in the Bible. You can say New Covenant rather than New Testament, but it is not necessary.

9. What experience have you had in sharing your faith with Jewish people?

Answer: Encourage people in your group to be honest and share their experiences. Most people have not had the courage to share with Jews thinking that the Jewish person knows a great deal more about the Holy Scriptures than they do. They also have not felt that it was "their job" since they weren't in full-time ministry. By your words, don't condemn anyone who has not yet witnessed, but rather encourage them to start fresh with their new understandings.

Understanding the Godhead

1. What does it mean when the New Testament says, "Unto the Jews I became as a Jew, that I might gain the Jews ... that I might by all means save some?"

Answer: Gentile believers do not become Jews, but "as

a Jew." We are to understand how Jewish people feel because of their suffering. Their lack of knowledge of what the Bible says must instill in us a love for them and desire to share God's Word. Much patience is needed. The Spirit of God will give us patience and understanding.

2. What do Jewish people believe about God?

    Answer: What Jews believe about God depends on what group in Judaism they attend and practice. Orthodox and Conservative Jews believe in God. The Reform and Reconstructionist usually do not. You will learn what they believe as you talk with them. If Jews say they believe in God, just what they believe can vary greatly.

3. Why is it important to know the Hebrew word for God and what it means in Genesis 1:1?

    Answer: Bible-believers can show from Genesis 1:1 the Hebrew word for God that reveals himself to us as a Unity (or Trinity). In Hebrew, when "im" is added to a word it makes it plural. The singular for God is El or Elah. In Genesis 1:1 the Hebrew word for God is *Elohim*—plural! Many verses in the Old Testament reveal to us that God is more than a single one. He is a Unity.

4. What does Genesis 1:1, 1:26 and 3:22 teach us about God?

    Answer: These Bible verses show us that God is a

Unity, for he speaks of himself as us, or our—all plural. This would be God the Father, God the Messiah/Son, and God the Holy Spirit (Genesis 1:2).

5. How would you explain what Isaiah 48:16–17 teaches about the Godhead?

Answer: The speaker in Isaiah 48:16 is God. The speaker is sent by the Lord God and His Spirit. Isaiah 48:17 makes clear the truth that the speaker is God who is also our Redeemer. The three members of the Godhead are given in these verses.

6. What do we learn about the Messiah from Jeremiah 23:5–6?

Answer: The LORD, who is God, will send to earth One who will reign and bring peace to Israel. The name of the One who is sent by the LORD is THE LORD OUR RIGHTEOUSNESS, or God! God sends God, or the second member of the Godhead.

7. What is the key verse in the Old Testament that Jews believe tells them that there is only one God? What does "echad" mean in this verse?

Answer: Deuteronomy 6:4 is the key verse in Judaism: "Hear, O Israel: the LORD our God is one LORD." "Our God" is the Hebrew *Elohenu*, which is the possessive form of *Elohim* and is plural. The Hebrew word for one is *echad*, which can be plural as in Genesis 2:24.

8. What is the Jewish prayer book?

Answer: The Jewish prayer book is called the "*Siddur.*" It is used for Jewish holy days and for weekly and daily times of worship.

The Two Comings of Messiah

1. What does Judaism teach regarding the person of the Messiah? Who is he? What is his relationship to the God of Israel?

    Answer: Jewish people who are Orthodox, Hasidic, and Conservative will usually believe that Messiah will be a great human leader. They do not believe that the Messiah is God. They do not associate any spiritual victory with the Messiah. Jews have never seen the Old Testament prophecies regarding the Messiah and what he would accomplish as a member of the Godhead.

2. What is the Jewish teaching concerning the coming of the Messiah? What will the Messiah accomplish for Israel?

    Answer: Orthodox, Hasidic, and perhaps Conservative Jews believe in the coming of the Messiah to bring peace to Israel. Their Messiah would be a leader like Moses to bring physical deliverance from oppression. Reform and Reconstructionist Jews usually believe in a "Messianic Era" when the world will get better and better until there is world peace. This is by human effort alone.

3. The Bible foretells how many comings of the Messiah to earth? Give scriptural substantiation for your answer.

   Answer: The Messiah comes two times to earth. His first coming is foretold in Isaiah 7:14, Micah 5:2, and Isaiah chapter 53 as well as other scriptures. Messiah's second coming to earth is given in Zechariah 14:1–4, 12:10, Jeremiah 23:5–6, Daniel 9:24–27 and other scriptures.

4. What will Messiah accomplish when he comes to earth?

   Answer: Messiah's first coming is to provide the blood of atonement by his death and resurrection for people to be forgiven of their sin—personal peace. This is for all who believe and trust him. After he accomplishes redemption for Jews and Gentiles, Messiah Jesus ascends to heaven—Psalm 110:1. Messiah Jesus is seated in heaven today awaiting his second coming to earth. The second coming is to defeat the world powers that have come against Israel at the end of the Great Tribulation period. After this great victory, Messiah Jesus will reign on earth and bring peace—world peace.

5. Will understanding the comings of the Messiah to earth assist you in sharing the gospel with lost souls, especially Jewish people? Explain your answer.

   Answer: The Jews who believe Messiah will come to bring peace to the world will not accept Jesus as

Messiah. Since Jesus did not bring peace to Israel and the world, they say Jesus cannot be the Messiah. This is a valid argument for those who do not know about the two comings of Messiah to earth. A careful Bible explanation of the two comings of Messiah can lead Jewish people to faith and salvation in Jesus.

6. What is the greatest prophetic chapter in the Bible about Messiah? How can you use it?

    Answer: Isaiah 53 is the greatest prophetic chapter about Messiah. It was written about seven hundred years before Christ and gives a complete picture of who the Messiah is and what he would accomplish for Jews and Gentiles. Be certain to read the twelve verses in this chapter to your Jewish friend and then go over it verse by verse.

7. What verses in the Old Testament foretell the first time Messiah comes?

    Answer: Daniel 9:24–27 is a great prophecy concerning the time when the Messiah would come to earth to die to provide the blood of atonement for lost souls. The years involved in this prophecy lead seeking hearts to Messiah Jesus' atonement that he provided in a d 32–33. Other events are also foretold to show the Bible is the word of Almighty God.

Amazing Prophecies about Jesus

1. How do we explain prophecy in the Old Testament? What is it?

    Answer: Prophecy is the foretelling of future events by the God of Israel through the Jewish men of God (Jewish prophets) who recorded these future events. The fulfillment of these prophecies confirms the Bible as the inspired words of Almighty God. People can put their faith in the Bible for it is true!

2. Why should we use prophecies when sharing the gospel?

    Answer: Fulfilled prophecy shows the Bible accounts are accurate and people can trust all that they read in the Holy Scriptures. Through fulfilled prophecy (Isaiah 53 and others), we know that Jesus is the promised Messiah and Redeemer. Through faith in Messiah Jesus we can be forgiven of our sins, have peace now and know that death is the doorway to eternity in heaven. This assurance brings wonderful peace!

3. What are the two major prophecies about the coming of Messiah in the Jewish Bible? Can sharing these prophecies actually lead a Jewish person to faith in Jesus? Practice sharing these prophecies with someone in your group or a friend.

    Answer: Isaiah 53 and Daniel 9:24–27 are the two main prophecies, but others are very important and complete the picture for unbelievers to see that Jesus is their Messiah. We have used these prophecies in witnessing to lead Jewish people to faith in Jesus. If possible, take time to break the group into smaller groups of 2 or 3 so that they can practice explaining the prophecies in their own words.

4. What key Scripture verses precede Isaiah 53? What do these verses tell us?

    Answer: Isaiah 52:13–15 sheds light on what is said in Isaiah 53. It is good to share these verses that explain how Messiah will die for our sins to be forgiven.

5. Explain briefly how you can share Isaiah 53.

    Answer: Turn in your Bible to Isaiah 53 and go over it verse by verse. Do this with someone in your small group or audibly to yourself if you are alone. If your study of these verses in Isaiah 53 is not sufficient for you to comfortably share the truths presented, go over the verses again. The time you spend to memorize the basic teaching of this chapter in God's Word will produce spiritual fruit in Jewish hearts.

6. How do Rabbis and Judaism interpret Isaiah 53 and how can you refute it?

    Answer: If this chapter comes up for discussion, remember that Jewish people are taught that Isaiah 53 speaks of Israel or the Jewish people. Isaiah 52:13–15 and Isaiah 53 are not recommended in the Jewish scripture readings, so Jews do not know these portions of the Bible. When you share the verses and the Jewish interpretation is mentioned (though this will be very seldom) a quick reference to verses in the chapter clearly shows the "he" cannot refer to the Jewish people. If they did, there would be no Jews alive today and the nation of Israel would not exist, for "he" dies so Jewish people can be forgiven of their sins. Refer to our notes for a detailed explanation.

When Will Messiah Come?

1. What do we learn from Daniel 9:25–26 about Messiah? Did Jesus fulfill these prophecies? What other main prophecy in Isaiah should you use with these verses in Daniel 9?

    Answer: In Daniel 9:25–26 we are told that a commandment would be given to rebuild Jerusalem which was in ruins. From that date, there would follow 483 years after which the Messiah would be cut off for the sins of the people. The book of Nehemiah gives the account of when the commandment was given to rebuild Jerusalem and the wall. The beginning of the years of this prophecy was 445 bc according to Nehemiah 2. When the years (360 days a year in the Jewish calendar) are counted down, the time of Messiah being cut-off comes out to when Jesus died for our sins. We find the words "cut-off" in Isaiah 53:8 foretelling the death of the Messiah as our sin-bearer. This prophecy also says that the Jewish temple and Jerusalem, which had been rebuilt, would be destroyed again just after the Messiah dies. The temple and Jerusalem were destroyed in a d 70.

2. When was this prophecy recorded? Is this a useful tool to share God's word with the unsaved? Why?

    Answer: Daniel 9:25–26 was recorded about 538 bc. About ninety-three years later, the book of Nehemiah gives the date when the prophecy began to be fulfilled in 445 bc. The fulfillment of Bible prophecy assures us of the accuracy of God's Word. This is vital for the unsaved to know, for they can trust God's plan of redemption in Jesus.

3. Who were Nehemiah and King Artaxerxes? How do they enter into this prophecy?

    Answer: Nehemiah was the Jewish man of God through whom the Lord worked to see this prophecy begin to be fulfilled. King Artaxerxes was the ruler whom God moved upon to give the commandment for Nehemiah to return to Jerusalem to rebuild the city and the wall about the city.

4. What future events are foretold in Daniel 9:24 and 9:27? How should these events influence our living today?

    Answer: Verse 24 foretells events (world peace) that will happen at a time that is yet in the future. These events will come upon the earth after what will happen in verse 27. Daniel 9:27 tells us that a world ruler (not the Messiah, but another ruler) will make a covenant with Israel to permit the Jewish people to worship in their rebuilt temple for seven years. We know this for this ruler breaks his promise to Israel and in the middle of the seven years, he stops the temple worship and sacrifices. Following this there will be much desolation. In Daniel 12:11–12 we see the time given in days from when the temple is polluted in the middle of the seven until the end of the seven. The total days reveal that from the middle of the seven until the end of the seven is just over 3–1/2 years. The total seven is then seven years. People who live longer than the seven years are blessed for they did not perish in the desolation. The prophecy in Zechariah 14 reveals that the Messiah will return to earth to defeat this ruler and his armies that have come against Jerusalem to destroy all the Jewish people. Daniel 9:24 is then fulfilled when Messiah Jesus brings peace to Jerusalem, the Jewish people and the world. We are living today in the days before Daniel 9:27 is fulfilled and this evil world ruler controls the world. The Lord is giving us time to share the gospel with lost souls before it is too late. Let us be faithful in our witness for Christ Jesus.

5. Do you have a clear understanding of what Daniel 9:24–27 foretells and can you use it to witness for the Lord?

Answer: If you do not understand this great prophecy, ask the Lord to show you the truth given to us in these verses of Scripture. God will help you and give you an effective witness to lost souls.

6. Does human history confirm the accuracy of Bible prophecy?

    Answer: Yes, it does! The events foretold in Daniel 9:25–26 have come to pass. Isaiah 53 has been fulfilled in Jesus. The Bible is God's word to us, and it is true!

The Bible

1. Do most Jews and Gentiles believe in God and the Bible? Why?

    Answer: In our experience these many years in the ministry, we have found that most Jews and Gentiles do not have an active faith in God and the Bible. They might have some belief in God, but it is not what the Bible teaches concerning Almighty God. Most people also have some respect for the Bible, but they do not accept the truths of the Holy Scriptures to be relevant to their living. Unfortunately, people base their opinions about the Bible and God on the basis of what they have seen in the lives of so-called Christians. This situation should affect true Christians and urge them to be effective witnesses for the Lord and the Bible. Many lost souls can be brought to faith in Christ Jesus by the faithful sharing of the gospel by loving Bible-believers. Lack of knowledge of just what the Bible says in the Old Testament and the New Testament is a major factor in the lives of Jewish and Gentile unbelievers today. It is our responsibility to give them the knowledge they need to put their faith in God's plan for their lives.

2. What two things are necessary for an effective witness? Romans 10:1.

Answer: A heart's desire to share the gospel with Jews and Gentiles and prayer to God for guidance in witnessing are essential for an effective ministry to lost souls. We need more than head knowledge.

3. What three basic truths can you share to show the Bible is true?

Answer: Sharing internal evidence, external evidence, and personal experience can be effective means for leading souls to faith in the Lord.

4. What is internal evidence? Give Scriptural references.

Answer: Internal evidence would be fulfilled prophecy. Sharing Isaiah 53, Daniel 9:24–27, Isaiah 7:14, Micah 5:2, and other prophecies will show that the Bible is true.

5. What is external evidence? Give two illustrations.

Answer: External evidence is the findings of archaeologists that confirm the biblical records of people, events, nations, etc. Isaiah 20:1 mentions

King Sargon. This king was not mentioned in secular history, and atheists said that the Bible was wrong and could not be trusted. Archaeologist Paul Botta in the mid 1800s, during an archaeological dig near Khorsabad on the north edge of Ninevah, found treasures, inscriptions, King Sargon's name, and his palace. The Bible is correct and trustworthy! In 2002, archaeologists in Jordan found the remains of Edom, a city mentioned in the days of King David and King Solomon but not in secular history. Critics of the Bible said the Bible was in error, but archaeologists' discoveries have proven the Bible is true.

6. What is personal experience? Give illustrations from the text and your life.

Answer: When a Jewish person or Gentile trusts the Bible as the Word of God and follows what God instructs us to do, there is real peace in that life for now and for eternity. At the funerals of George's wife Doris and Jean's husband Richard, there was peace because they were Bible-believers and George and Jean knew they were in heaven. God's peace for believers in this life, and for the assurance of heaven someday, is a wonderful testimony to lost souls.

7. How can you challenge an atheist to seek God?

Answer: Bible-believers, according to the Holy Scriptures, know their sins are forgiven and upon death will go to heaven. If the Bible is not true, then believers have lived a good life and, after they die, there will be nothing. The unbeliever will also die and there will be nothing. If the Bible is true, and we know it is, the Bible-believer will be in heaven, and the unbeliever will be in suffering forever in hell. Isn't it worth it for the unbeliever to investigate to see if the Bible is true?

8. Is the Jewish Bible arranged differently than your Bible? How?

Answer: Yes, the arrangement of the books in the Jewish Bible is different from other Bibles. The books are in a number of groupings, or categories. Each category has a table of contents, so you can thumb through the Bible until you find the category and book you are looking for. If you are sharing with an Orthodox Jew, it is possible that his Bible is in Hebrew. Just ask him to read from it and translate the verses into English. In a number of Jewish Bibles, you begin reading from the back to the front. Be prepared for this possibility.

9. Are all translations of the Bible the same? Why is this important?

Answer: All Jewish translations are not the same. Older versions of Jewish Bible are much like the King James Version. We use the KJV when we witness to Jewish people. Newer Jewish translations change words to conform to modern Judaism. For instance, hell is not used. The word convert in Psalm 51 is changed but has somewhat the same meaning.

When you witness, just share the Bible truths and ask the Spirit of God to make the truth real to the Jewish or Gentile inquirer.

Eternity
Part A—Heaven

1. Explain what the Jewish Bible teaches us about a real, literal heaven. Is there more than one heaven?

   Answer: Yes, the Jewish Bible, our Old Testament, presents the truth that heaven is a real place. Actually, the Bible speaks of three heavens with the highest heaven being the throne of God.

2. Who is in heaven?

   Answer: All believers, Jewish and Gentile, are now in heaven with God our heavenly Father, Christ Jesus, the Holy Spirit and all of the heavenly hosts.

3. What did God show to Moses on Mount Sinai?

   Answer: God showed Moses the tabernacle that is in heaven from which Moses was to make a copy.

4. What was the purpose of the Jewish tabernacle? Is there a tabernacle that means something to us? Explain your answer.

   Answer: The tabernacle was the place where the blood of atonement was offered once a year on the Day of Atonement (Leviticus 16). The tabernacle was also used for daily animal sacrifices for Jews to be forgiven of their sins (Leviticus 5:5–10). There is a tabernacle in heaven into which Messiah Jesus entered with his blood, after his death and resurrection, to place his blood there as a once for all time blood sacrifice to cleanse sinners of their sins. This means everything to us for our faith in Jesus' death and resurrection is effective for our salvation by his blood of atonement in the tabernacle in heaven (Hebrews 9 and Revelation 11:19, 15:5).

5. What Jewish people, whom we know from the Jewish Bible, had the assurance that they would see God in heaven after their death?

    Answer: In the Old Testament, we read about Job's faith in Job 19:25–27. Isaiah spoke of his resurrection from the grave in Isaiah 26:19. King David's faith brought peace for the future resurrection as recorded in Psalm 16:8–11. Remember the word hell in verse 10 is the Hebrew word *Sheol* that had two parts, one part for the righteous in peace and the other part for sinners and suffering.

6. How can Jews and Gentiles be certain of going to heaven when they die?

    Answer: Sin separates people from God for this life and for eternity in hell after death. Messiah (Christ) Jesus died on the cross to provide the cleansing blood of atonement for all who would believe in him. When a sinner confesses his sins to God and asks for God's cleansing with the blood of Jesus, that person is forgiven of all sin. All people who have been forgiven of their sins will go to heaven when they die. Read John 3:16, 1 Peter 1:3–9, and Colossians 1:12–14.

Part B—Hell

1. What will happen to people who die who have not trusted in God's plan of salvation?

   Answer: God's Word, the Bible, clearly tells us what happens to people who die with sin in their lives. God will judge sinners and sin will be punished in an everlasting hell.

2. What is *Sheol, Hades,* and *Gehenna?*

   Answer: *Sheol* is a Hebrew word found in the Old Testament that is usually translated hell in our Bibles. In Jewish translations, it might be translated hell or by other words that mean suffering after death. Many times it is translated the grave. *Sheol* in Old Testament times is the place to which people went after physical death. It had two parts, one for the righteous whose sins had been forgiven by God, and the other part for those who died with sin in their lives having never accepted God's plan for cleansing from sin. The righteous were living in peace while the sinners were in great suffering. People had all of their senses in *Sheol. Hades* is a Greek word that is translated hell in the New Testament. It is the same place as the Hebrew *Sheol.* A clear description of *Hades* is given in Luke 16:19–31. At the Great White Throne Judgment in Revelation 20:11–15, 21:8, sinners are taken from *Hades,* judged and then are cast into *Gehenna* which is the everlasting punishment in the lake of fire. When Jesus died and was resurrected, he went down to *Hades* and took the believers in the righteous part of *Hades* up with him to paradise or heaven.

3. What do Jewish people believe about hell? What does the Jewish prophet Isaiah tell us in Isaiah 33:14?

    Answer: Jewish people do not believe in hell. Their Bible does teach that there is such a place of suffering. Isaiah, the greatest of the Jewish prophets, recorded the Word of God in Isaiah 33:14, "The sinners in Zion are afraid; fearfulness hath surprised the hypocrites. Who among us shall dwell with the devouring fire? Who among us shall dwell with everlasting burnings?" Sinners will dwell or live in everlasting burnings that will devour or overcome them but not annihilate them. There are many Old Testament verses that teach us there is a place of suffering for sinners after death in *Sheol.*

4. What do we learn about *Sheol* and Pharoah and his army that is recorded by the Jewish prophet Ezekiel in 31:2, 31:16–17, 32:21 and 32:31?

    Answer: Pharoah and his army are slain in battle. After death they go down to *Sheol.* The army that slew

Pharoah and his army then die in battle. Pharoah, who is in *Sheol,* sees the death of his enemies and their coming to the place where he is. Pharoah, after his death and his descending to *Sheol,* sees the same thing happen to the army that caused his death and he is comforted, or glad, that this has happened. In *Sheol* Pharoah remembered, saw or had his sight, and had emotions. This is similar to the account of the sinner in *Hades* in Luke 16:19–31.

5. What does King David of Israel tell us about *Sheol* in Psalm 16:8–11?

Answer: King David was a righteous man who asked God for the forgiveness of his sins as he recorded it in Psalm 51. In Psalm 16:8–11 David states that he would have peace in *Sheol* but would leave there someday and be with God evermore. This would be heaven. King David had God's presence and fullness of joy!

6. In the New Testament, Jesus spoke of *Hades* and two men in Luke 16:19–31. What key truths do we learn from this passage of God's Word?

Answer: People, who confess their sin to God and trust him for salvation, will live in wonderful peace after death. This was the experience of Lazarus as he abode with Abraham. The rich man died without trusting God for the forgiveness of his sins, and he went to the suffering part of *Hades.* Lazarus, nor anyone else, could alleviate the suffering of the sinner. There is no second chance to be forgiven of sin once a person dies. We also learn that even if a person came back from the dead to warn sinners to repent, they would not believe. People must believe Moses and the prophets (who spoke about Messiah Jesus) to be forgiven of their sins.

7. What do we learn about *Gehenna* in Revelation 20:11–15 and 21:8?

Answer: *Gehenna* is the Greek name for eternal hell. It is a place of horrible pain and suffering in the lake of fire for those who reject Christ Jesus as their Savior and die in their sins.

8. Will what you learned about hell give you a greater burden to share the gospel with lost souls? Will you witness for Jesus?

Answer: Only you can answer this question. Pray for the Lord to give you a burden for lost Jews and Gentiles and to open the way for you to witness to them.

9. Practice witnessing with someone in your shall group talking about heaven and hell.

If time permits, let participants break into smaller groups and practice witnessing to someone Jewish about heaven and hell. Encourage them to be open and honest in their sharing. If time does not permit, strongly encourage them to practice at home. At your next meeting, encourage them to share with a partner the words they would use. If you are reading this book by yourself, find a friend who will give you an honest critique. The more you practice, the more comfortable you will become with the appropriate words and phrases in witnessing to the Jews.

Special Tracts and CDs for Your Witness

1. What are some differences in the tracts you distribute to Gentiles and to Jews?

   Answer: There can be a great difference between the tracts that you usually give to Gentile lost souls and the tracts that you should give to Jewish people. Tracts you pick up at church might have words in them like Lord Christ Jesus, Christian, cross, Trinity, etc. These words should not be used in tracts for Jews. The tracts should say Messiah Jesus instead of Lord Christ Jesus, Bible-believer instead of Christian, the place where Jesus died for us to be forgiven of our sins instead of cross, the Godhead instead of Trinity, etc. Using the right tracts can be a helpful in witnessing to Jewish people.

2. Are Jewish people, according to Judaism, Jewish if their father or mother is Jewish?

   Answer: To a modern Jew, they are Jewish if both parents were Jews or at least the mother was Jewish. The Old Testament teaches that being a Jew is determined by the father.

3. What tracts are available to you to give to Jewish

inquirers? Is there a good way to distribute tracts and CDs?

Answer: Several tracts have been written by George Gruen. These are "Peace in these Times," "Who Is a Jew?" and "Have You Discovered the Principles for Personal Peace?" We have also recorded four CDs that contain key messages. The tracts and CDs are available by using the contact information at the end of this book. It is easy to leave a tract with a Jewish person. Just say, "I know a Jewish man who has a relationship with the God of Israel that has given him great peace. He has written this leaflet (or recorded this CD). I will leave it with you. The next time I see you let me know what you think about it." Place the tract or CD on a table and leave. Use a similar approach with your doctor, dentist, or pharmacist. Do not hand it to the person, for then he or she can refuse to accept it.

4. Is there a tract for Jewish people designed for you to read and discuss with them? Explain.

Answer: "Have You Discovered the Principles for Personal Peace?" is available in large print. This tract can be shared with a Jewish friend or a couple. Place the tract on a table and read through it slowly while making comments and answering questions. Practice ahead of time what your comments will be and anticipate how you will answer questions.

5. Is there a tract with large print that is good for people who cannot see very well to read?

    Answer: Our tract, "Have You Discovered the Principles for Personal Peace?" is available in a very large size. It is a good tract to give to a person who has vision problems, to one who is elderly or to use in a home situation or on a bus or airplane when you can sit and go through the tract. Practice reading the tract with another Christian.

6. Share how you will use tracts and CDs to reach Jewish people with the gospel.

    Answer: You can do it! There is much joy when you have the opportunity to share a tract with a lost soul. Ask the Lord to open ways for you to witness with the use of a tract or CD. Encourage participants to share specific ways they can and will use a tract or CD to reach a lost soul with the gospel.

Making Openings to Share the Gospel

1. How can you share the gospel with a Jewish person who has married someone in your family?

    Answer: After you have sincerely and lovingly welcomed the Jewish man or woman into your family and have established a mutual friendship, you can share God's word. An opening can be made by saying, "David, I have known you for sometime now and there is something that I would like to share with you and get your opinion. A Jewish man I know has a great relationship with the God of Israel that has given him real peace. He has written this leaflet (or recorded this CD), and I would really appreciate your opinion of it. The next time I see you and we have some free time, let me know what you think about it, thanks." Put the tract or CD on a table or hand it to him and then leave.

2. Explain how you can share a tract with a Jewish neighbor.

Answer: You can share your faith with a neighbor by giving her a tract in a similar way that you would with a Jewish relative. With a neighbor, you could ask if she has some free time to come over for a cup of coffee. Tell her you have something to share with her/him that is very interesting and you would like her opinion. In your home, read through the large-print tract "Have You Discovered the Principles for Personal Peace?"

3. Is there a way that you can give God's Word to your doctor or pharmacist? Share how you can give the gospel to someone at work.

Answer: We have discussed sharing a tract with a professional person in our study on special tracts and CDs. You can use the same approach with someone at work. There might be the opportunity to share a tract at lunch hour. If not, offer the tract or CD as lunch is ending and place the tract on the table. Ask your co-worker to look it over that night and to let you know the next day what he or she thought of it. You might also have opportunity to share as you leave the store or office.

4. Is there a tract or booklet that can be given to a college or university student?

Answer: The tract "Have You Discovered the Principles for Personal Peace?" comes in a small size that is good for college and university students. Leave this tract with a student the same way you would with a professional person. It is possible, if the student expresses interest right away or asks questions, that you might have the opportunity to explain the tract there on campus. Go over the tract page by page and point by point.

5. Can a witness be given to high school students? How?

Answer: With conditions in public schools today, if you are a student it might be best to wait until you are off the school grounds and then offer the small principles tract the way you would with a professional person. There are circumstances when you might be able to have time to witness. Use the small tract and go through it with your Jewish friend or Gentile friend. For Gentiles, you should find some good gospel tracts at your church.

6. Can you be a testimony in public transportation, terminals, or restaurants? Explain.

Answer: When you are sitting next to a person who is not reading, take the large-print tract and slowly go through it page by page. Give the person next to you time to look over and see what you are reading. The tract is sufficiently large for a person nearby to read it along with you! Use this tract when you are in a restaurant. Many people read the newspaper when they have breakfast, lunch, or dinner. Pray someone will see the tract and ask you questions.

7. What other ways can we get the gospel to lost souls?

Answer: Many years ago, we had basketball and baseball teams for the sole purpose of inviting unsaved Jewish young men to join our teams. With each ballgame, we had a Bible discussion after the game at our home or even on the ball field. We were in city leagues most of the time but also in a church league for basketball. As a result, souls were saved. You can have a literature display at a country fair or in a shopping mall. There are small stands that will give you a great opportunity to display tracts and Christian literature. We mixed the Jewish tracts with tracts for Gentiles. Many people stopped and asked questions. There are many groups that have tract distribution on the sidewalks in cities. This can be in a neighborhood of your choice. You no doubt will have to have a permit or at least look into it. This is a good way to reach hundreds and even thousands of souls with the gospel. There will be many who ask questions. There might be people who are antagonistic, but this can be expected.

Understanding the Faith of Jewish People

1. What books are in the Jewish Bible? What is the Jewish Talmud?

    Answer: There are thirty-nine books in the Jewish Bible just as there are in your Old Testament; however, the order is different. Jewish Bibles that are in Hebrew and English could read from the back to the front. Other Jewish Bibles read as ours—front to back. Jewish Bibles have a number of sections with books listed in each section. You will have to thumb through their Bible if you have to read from it. If the Jewish person does not ask you to read from his or her Bible, just read from your own. I recommend the King James Version for it is the best translation when looking up prophecy Scriptures. One Jewish version, now out of print, was word for word like the KJV in many verses. The Talmud is a collection of writings constituting Jewish civil and religious law. The Talmud has two sections, the Mishnah and the Gemarah. Many Jewish people are taught that when God gave the Law to Moses, there was also an oral law given that was handed down through the generations until around a d 200. It was put into writings called the Mishnah. Rabbis made commentaries on the Mishnah and called these writings the Gemarah.

The Talmud has many volumes. Many Jews know nothing or very little about the Talmud even as they know very little about the Bible.

2. What are Orthodox Jews? What do they believe?

   Answer: Orthodox Jews are very religious and adhere to the traditions and rites of older Judaism. They meet in synagogues and wear special attire. They would accept the Talmud as being equal with the Bible. They attempt to keep the Law of Moses and would accept their Bible as being from God. They believe Messiah will come to bring peace to Israel and the world. To them, Jesus is a Jewish prophet but not the Messiah and not the Son of God. Orthodox Jews have no assurance of going to heaven when they die.

3. What are Hasidic Jews? What is their faith?

   Answer: Hasidic Jews are very zealous and ardent in their relationship to God. Prayer is a central part of their lives and is motivated by their love for God. They consider themselves to be very Jewish.

4. Compare Conservative Judaism to the Orthodox and Hasidic.

   Answer: Conservative Jews observe traditional forms of worship but will modify them to make them relevant to modern living. The practices of Conservative Judaism are between the Orthodox and the Reform. They are not as strict as the Orthodox and not as liberal as the Reform.

5. What do we know about Reform Judaism?

Answer: These are Jews of the Reform persuasion and not reformed. The word synagogue has been replaced by temple as their place of worship. They teach that nations can achieve peace without God or the Messiah. Many are atheists or agnostics. They stress brotherhood, humanity, and a life of good deeds. They are not concerned about sin, heaven, or hell.

6. What do Jews of the Reconstructionist faith believe?

Answer: The Reconstructionists began in Philadelphia, Pennsylvania, in the 1900s. They are concerned with the here and now and find no meaning in a personal God. They reject the supernatural and miracles. They believe in good deeds. They do not accept the Bible as the Word of God for they do not believe in God.

7. Briefly explain the Jewish holy days and holidays of Passover, New Year, Day of Atonement, and *Hanukkah*. How can we witness to Jews during these special days?

Answer: Passover is the Jewish celebration, usually in April, that remembers the deliverance of the Jewish people from Egyptian bondage. There are special family dinners with significance given to what happened in Egypt and on the night of Passover. It is a joyous time for the children of Israel. *Rosh Hashanah* is the Jewish New Year that comes in September or October. It is the beginning of ten days of heart searching for Jewish people in preparation for *Yom Kippur*, the Day of Atonement on the tenth day after *Rosh Hashanah*. Jewish people seek God for the forgiveness of their sins on the Day of Atonement by fasting, praying and giving to support their synagogue. They have no assurance of the forgiveness of their sins for they have no blood of atonement as God required in Leviticus 16. The blood of atonement is found today in Messiah Jesus as God foretold in Isaiah 53 and other Scriptures. Jewish people need to hear the message of redemption in Jesus. *Hanukkah* is in December and is a joyous celebration of the victory of Maccabeus and the Jewish people in a war over the Syrians in 168–165 bc. The Syrians had captured Jerusalem, desecrated the temple, and wanted to destroy Judaism and everything connected with the Jews. God's miracle, through the Jewish army, defeated the Syrians. The polluted temple in Jerusalem was recaptured and rededicated. This holiday is also called the Feast of Dedication. It is an eight-day celebration with gifts exchanged during the days. *Hanukkah* is a good time to share your faith in Messiah Jesus for we might not have our faith had there not been the victory in 165 bc. The Old Testament was preserved for us with the prophecies about Messiah Jesus and redemption in him.

Relationships with New Jewish Believers

1. Will new Jewish believers in Jesus suffer persecution because of their faith? Who will foster this persecution? Why?

   Answer: Jewish people, who accept Jesus as their Messiah and Savior, might suffer opposition to their new faith. This can be expected and the believer should be prepared to answer questions from their family. The opposition can come from family members, relatives, and friends. Jews have suffered so much at the hands of so-called Christians that it is very difficult for them to accept a Jewish person who believes in Jesus.

2. How can persecution and opposition be overcome?

   Answer: Persecution and opposition can be overcome by prayer, sharing the truth of God as given in the Bible for Jewish people, and assuring those involved that a Jewish person, who accepts Jesus as Messiah and Redeemer, is still Jewish. The problem that unbelievers have is that, for the most part, they have little or no knowledge of what the God of Israel expects of the children of Israel. We must make every effort to acquaint them with what the Old Testament says about sin, heaven and hell, and what comes after death. Jewish people need to know what the will of Almighty God is for Jews.

3. How can new believers grow in grace? What are two essentials for their new life in Jesus.

Answer: New believers, be they Jewish or Gentile, must be urged to read the Bible daily. Faith comes by reading the Word of God. Suggest that they read Hebrews, Matthew, Galatians, Ephesians, Philippians, and Colossians. This will give them a good foundation for their faith. Always give them answers for their questions. If you do not have an answer, go to your pastor or other teacher in your church or contact us. The second essential for every new believer is to learn to pray. Most people who put their trust in Jesus will have no idea of how to pray. Teach them by example. Pray with them. Help them to understand that prayer is talking with God, and he hears their prayers.

4. What about church attendance? Small group meetings? Should they attend Jewish religious services and holidays? What will you say to a new believer as you bring him/her to your church?

Answer: It might take time for a Jewish believer to attend church. This is all new to them. They will need to understand what it means and what will be done in the services. It should be fine to invite the new one in Jesus to attend a small group during the week or on Sunday evening in someone's home. Make them feel at home by your love and care for them. When Jewish believers are grounded in the Word of God, it should be all right for them to attend a special Jewish holiday service. By their attendance, they will show their family that they are still Jews. Such services would be at Passover and Hanukkah. If your church has a cross in the Sanctuary, make sure you explain its significance.

5. Who is a Goy? What does this mean to a Jewish believer?

    Answer: A Goy is a Gentile. For many Jews, a Goy would also be a Christian. A Jewish believer would not want to be called a Goy. The Jewish family members might call him or her a Goy, but the believer must tell them that he or she is not a Goy but is still a Jew. The Jewish believers have put their faith in the God of Israel and the Jewish Messiah with the blood of atonement that is promised in the Jewish Bible. This is not a Gentile faith but it is Jewish from the God of Israel. Jewish believers in Messiah Jesus are actually more Jewish than many members of their families who do not believe in God or the Bible.

6. What are some family arguments against new believers?

    Answer: Family members will say the believers are traitors to the Jewish people. They will be accused of making members of the family sick, especially the parents and grandparents. Though the believers are very intelligent with perhaps a good college education, they will be called stupid. Their faith will be called an embarrassment to family members when the community learns that they believe in Jesus. Material and financial enticements might be offered to draw the believers away from their new faith in Jesus. There will be many, many accusations and arguments from unbelievers to try to turn the new Bible-believers back to what would be called their Jewish heritage. Jewish people do not give up their heritage when they trust in Messiah Jesus. Believers in Jesus are still Jews and sometimes more Jewish than before. What they do give up is Judaism's system of good works to try to be forgiven of their sins. Salvation is found in trusting Jesus as Messiah and Redeemer. His shed blood is the blood of atonement for our sins to be forgiven by God. Opposition to the new believers' faith in Jesus can be overcome by prayer and by sharing encouragement from the Bible. As you continue to study this book, you will learn how to relate to Jewish people who have put their trust in Messiah Jesus. Your understanding of the opposition they are going through, and your love and guidance to support them, will mean much toward giving them a solid foundation for their faith in the Lord.

Contact Information

For pricing information on any of the tracts or CDs mentioned in this book, please write to George and Jean Gruen at P.O. Box 97, Ephrata, PA 17522–0097 or contact them via email at contact@sharinggodstruth.org. You can also order tracts or CDs via their website at www. sharinggodstruth.org.

Bibliography

The Holy Scriptures, Translated by Alexander Harkavy, Hebrew Publishing Company, Vol. 2, Page 673, 1916.